P9-CDE-939

TOURO COLLEGE LIBRARY
Kings Hwy

WITHDRAWN

Conflict Resolution Communication

Patterns Promoting Peaceful Schools

TOURO COLLEGE LIBRARY
Kings Hwy

Melinda Lincoln

A SCARECROWEDUCATION BOOK

The Scarecrow Press, Inc.
Lanham, Maryland, and London
2002

KH

A SCARECROW EDUCATION BOOK

Published in the United States of America
by Scarecrow Press, Inc.
A Member of the Rowman & Littlefield Publishing Group
4720 Boston Way, Lanham, Maryland 20706
www.scarecroweducation.com

4 Pleydell Gardens, Folkestone
Kent CT20 2DN, England

Copyright © 2002 by Melinda Lincoln

All rights reserved. No part of this publication may be reproduced,
stored in a retrieval system, or transmitted in any form or by any
means, electronic, mechanical, photocopying, recording, or otherwise,
without the prior permission of the publisher.

British Library Cataloguing in Publication Information Available

Library of Congress Cataloging-in-Publication Data
Lincoln, Melinda, 1948–
   Conflict resolution communication : patterns promoting peaceful schools / Melinda
Lincoln.
      p. cm.
   Includes bibliographical references and index.
   ISBN 0-8108-4388-9 (alk. paper)
   ISBN 0-8108-4264-5 (paper : alk. paper)
      1. Communication in education—United States. 2. Conflict management—Study
and teaching—United States. 3. School violence—United States—Prevention.   I. Title.

LB1033.5 .L56 2002
371.5—dc21

                                                                    2001057704

∞™ The paper used in this publication meets the minimum requirements of
American National Standard for Information Sciences-Permanence of
Paper for Printed Library Materials, ANSI/NISO Z39.48-1992.
Manufactured in the United States of America.

10/25/04

I wish to honor the memory of those who lost their lives in the tragedy that startled the safety of the nation on September 11, 2001, by dedicating this text to them. May their friends and families find comfort in having known the embrace of great heroes and may the world once again find strength in peaceful resolution.

Contents

Foreword

There was a time, and not that long ago, when the only behavior problems most teachers faced were students' chewing gum in class or smoking in the restrooms. Occasionally, a fistfight would break out on the playground that was short and ended after a few blows. No one ever went home to steal their father's pistol and return to school to seek deadly vengeance.

Those were different times and in many ways better times. Not that we should glorify the "good old days." They had their problems as well—one of them being that public education either by design or for reasons beyond its control was elitist. A hundred years ago, only 10 percent of youngsters finished high school. Many young boys dropped out to work for money that was needed at home. Many young girls quit schooling to help out at home. Children from well-to-do families had better opportunities to finish high school. Today, some 90 percent of our children complete high school. Our educational system reflects a society that is dramatically more diverse than in years gone by.

Conflict among human beings has always existed and probably always will. But in generations past, serious conflicts were the domain of adults not children. Parents could rest assured that schools were among the safest institutions of our society. Our present inability to address conflict in a nonviolent "win-win" fashion has doomed us to our destructive reality. It is rare that a week goes by without yet another news story about violence in our schools and colleges.

A reality that can—as Dr. Melinda Lincoln so adroitly points out in this timely book—be changed.

Communications

Human resource experts tell us that most human conflicts are based on a lack of communication. People fail to clearly state what is expected, others do not understand the instructions, and others understand but resist them for any number of reasons . . . and on and on. Psychologists note that behavior modification is not possible without a clear line, a two-way line, of communication. Finally, historians tell us that war erupts when diplomacy fails and that good communication does not exist.

Clearly for conflict to be addressed and resolved, effective communication is absolutely essential. That truism is clearly established and reinforced over and over again in this book. It is fortuitous that Dr. Lincoln is an expert in both communication and in conflict resolution. But that statement may be criticized for being redundant because as she so clearly points out throughout the book—conflict cannot be resolved without communication.

The book is written in a logical and systematic fashion. The reader is introduced to the problem and then is led carefully to a series of solutions. It becomes clear early on that many participants have to come together to succeed, that learned behavior from those that we love and respect may sometimes be counterindicated and destructive. The process to be followed to succeed has many ramifications.

The problem of conflict is not a simple one and simplistic superficial solutions will not work. Dr. Lincoln has developed a logical process, a path that can be followed. Every paragraph in this book is thoughtful and thought provoking. One finds oneself shaking one's head and sighing, "Ah, yes." Or "That's so true. Why didn't I think of that?"

As the author wisely points out, conflict resolution communication is a process, a journey, not a solution to be learned once and then forgotten. Conflict resolution solutions are ever changing and developing phenomena. The lesson is never fully learned for we are dealing with human beings and all the complexities they represent. They change, situations change, but the landmark lessons so carefully detailed in this book can help us deal with old patterns and new problems we haven't even dreamed of yet.

Conflict Resolution Communication: Patterns Promoting Peaceful Schools
is well researched, well written, and ever so timely.

Gustavo A. Mellander, Ph.D.
Professor and Dean Emeritus
Graduate School of Education
George Mason University

Preface

As the proverbial student, no matter where I am in my life, learning never takes a backseat. I ponder and try to understand the ways of the world: people interacting with one another, communicating in like fashion, and attempting to respond to what is being stated rather than what is being heard within one's own frame of reference. The daily dilemma of miscommunication or conflicted situations between people is bound to repeat itself hundreds of times before our eyes grow weary and yearn for slumber. Confused states of interaction exist between people in the home, at work, and in the community, but gaining a sharper focus of understanding, depth, and communication of thought is the key to alleviating the effects and the traumas of ambivalence, turmoil, and chaos.

My world of conflict resolution communication invites professionals, students, parents, friends, relatives, bosses, co-workers, teachers, health-care technicians, grocery store clerks, in-laws, siblings, cousins, computer specialists, auto workers, laborers, pilots, dependents, engineers, airline servers, delivery persons, truck drivers, florists, children, teens, professors, captains, deans, military personnel, presidents, news anchors, and talk-show hosts to solve their problems, troubles, and altercations peacefully by using effective devices and techniques offered in the context of this book.

By successfully blending the processes of communication and mediation practices, you can productively lessen routine strife and learn new patterns of behavior to solve differences without violence. The effective employment of interactive communication processes, including listening skills, eye-to-eye contact, gestures, conversation, and body language, comprises an essential element of the total program. The effectiveness of my program depends on a successful blending of fundamental communication theories in combination with the rudiments of conflict resolution practices. By isolating issues, moving heated emotions aside, demonstrating tolerance and respect for others, learning to apply empathy, acknowledging other points of view, and working towards compromise and negotiation, we achieve a "win-win" atmosphere of cooperation and a desire to reduce conflict for the betterment of all.

My hope is that after reading *Conflict Resolution Communication: Promoting Peaceful Schools*, you, too, will find it easier to identify and to change old behavior patterns, and that these changes will introduce new concepts and ways of improving your interaction with family, friends, and acquaintances. With that goal in mind, I humbly submit my thought patterns, verbal articulation, and an insider's perspective of conflict resolution communication strategies for a richer, fuller, and more peaceful tomorrow.

Acknowledgments

Conflict Resolution Communication: Promoting Peaceful Schools is a labor of love intended to empower future generations to skillfully work through conflict and cultural diversity without violence or inappropriate behaviors. I would like to recognize my parents, who instilled the love of learning within me; my family and friends, who believed in me; my professors, teachers, colleagues, and students, who inspired me to continuously grow; and Oxford, where I found myself and learned to exist in a world that took my breath away.

Universal Declaration of Communication Principles 1999–2002

The following Principles of Communication were composed by my hand on the 11th day of November 1999, at the University of Oxford, in Oxford, England. I wish to honor each and every individual with the rights, the privileges, and the interactive communication and free expression of thought inherent to all mankind.

As I completed my doctoral studies as a graduate resident, I reflected on the theories of interaction among peoples of all cultures. These standards of communication are intrinsically incorporated into the rudiments and practices of Conflict Resolution Communication.

PREAMBLE

Whereas recognition of the inherent dignity and of the equal and inalienable rights of all members of the human family is the foundation of interactive communication, and free expression of thought.

Whereas it is essential to guarantee the right of freedom of opinion and expression to all mankind.

Whereas it is essential to promote language usage and public communication including freedom to hold opinions without interference and to seek, receive, and impart information and ideas through any media and regardless of frontiers.

Now, Therefore, This UNIVERSAL DECLARATION OF COMMUNICATION PRINCIPLES will be accepted as a common standard of expression, thought, opinion, and interactive discourse among participants, speakers, and listeners based on cooperation principles, speaker credibility, reason, facts, evidence, and the effects of the message on society as a whole.

Article 1.
To become "cooperative language users" without covertly exploiting or flounting expressions of communication.

Article 2.
To maintain a natural discourse or conversation of "ordinary language."

Article 3.
To present clear sentences and truth values free from Metaphysical Implicatures, identification of subject-items, and predicate categories.

Article 4.
To analyze and explicate the meaning of expressions.

Article 5.
To recognize valid inferences and arguments.

Article 6.
To provide clarification and definition for analysis and logical equivalent.

Article 7.
To provide conversational interaction and face-to-face discourse.

Article 8.
To understand implicature by determining what is implicated or said.

Article 9.
To recognize the importance of context and background information.

Article 10.
To recognize nondetachability by what was said and not rely on virtue of the manner of expression.

Article 11.
To divert from long-winded conversation or artificial in manner.

Article 12.
To recognize words through meaning, context, and having a choice when possible.

Article 13.
To recognize that whole language is a matter of meeting the listener's expectations of cooperation.

Article 14.
To recognize the relevance of whole language theory in understanding language, logic, and conversational meaning.

Article 15.
To realize that the structure of the sentence serves as an image of the structure of the thought.

Article 16.
To recognize that the speaker intends for a meaning to be interpreted by the receiver.

Article 17.
To recognize that age, maturity, and various cultural elements of background and knowledge play a major role in discourse or areas of communication.

Article 18.
To realize that the user's competence or knowledge of the language and its rules may be contrasted to the practice of performance.

Article 19.
To recognize the importance and relevance of pragmatic theories explicating the reasoning of speakers and listeners.

Article 20.
To acknowledge the function of language as promoting expression, speech, representation, coding, channeling, and poetic quantity within the communication process.

Article 21.
To understand the fulfillment of communication functions in conversation, order, direction, purpose, verbalization, knowledge, learning, education, and interactive face-to-face language usage.

Article 22.
To realize that everyone has the right of freedom of expression, including the right of freedom to hold opinions and to receive and impart information and ideas without interference by public authority.

Article 23.
To promote the exercise of these freedoms in a democratic society.

Article 24.
To protect the moral character and reputation of others through proper language usage without the use of defamation, slander, or sedition in lowering a person's standing before others, or cause that person to be shunned or exposed to hatred, contempt, or ridicule.

Article 25.
To present ethical standards of communication based on sound reasoning, solid evidence, a commitment to truth, and a sense of social responsibility.

Article 26.
To practice liberty of speech by keeping viable a "marketplace of ideas" to supply citizens of a free society with essential information and a variety of viewpoints.

Article 27.
To promote a respect for persons and a preference for persuasion over coercion to develop a social policy based on standards of communication ethics.

Article 28.
To recognize that speech serves to strengthen the process of democracy, fosters the freedom of expression, provides information adequate for constructive decisions, engages in significant debate, examines alternatives and objectively appraises evidence and conclusions, and inspires to truth telling and noble objectives.

Article 29.
To encourage the enlightened use of communication by developing a respect for precision and accuracy in communication, and for reasoning based upon evidence and a judicious discrimination among values.

Article 30.
To encourage the role of well-informed and articulate citizens, to defend the communication rights of those with whom they may disagree, and to expose abuses of the communication process.

Article 31.
To utilize communication principles in a free interactive marketplace of ideas.

Introduction

Conflict Resolution Communication: Patterns Promoting Peaceful Schools is designed for professionals in the educational arena, including teachers, administrators, counselors, social workers, psychologists, parents, and students, who are looking for effective alternative practices in conflict resolution blended with successful communication skills. Too often, the process of mediation or voluntary agreement by the parties to work toward a solution and to resolve a conflict peacefully need to be addressed through communication techniques involving listening and hearing exercises, improvisations, role-play situations, and verbal narratives.

Parties involved in negotiating, compromising, and facilitating an acceptable agreement through conflict resolution communication tend to listen to the other person's point of view more carefully, appreciate the many sides of a disagreement more openly, and dissolve their anger and tarnished emotions more readily. Narrative mediation allows the participants to relay their individual stories or accounts leading up to the conflict in a safe environment without interruption, threats, harassment, or verbal accusations. By moving the emotions aside, identifying the issues, and focusing on the existing differences, the conflict resolution communication specialist or those trained in the process assist the parties to resolve the altercation, at hand, by brainstorming or problem-solving possible solutions leading to a "win-win" outcome for all concerned.

Conflict resolution communication is particularly effective within the school setting because students often do not identify the issues surrounding the conflict carefully. They may form opinions and thoughts, and engage in overheated emotions based on third-party involvement, hearsay, "he said/she said" accusations, lack of information, rumors, threats, and miscommunication between observers, informers, and the parties involved. Those "would-be" friends and loyal supporters for whatever reasons, at times, may do more harm than good by spreading unconfirmed, misquoted, and out-of-context information that quickly leads to shouting, bullying, pushing, shoving, and, most unfortunately, violence in schools. To encourage thinking before acting, talking before striking, and mediating differences before tragedy erupts on school campuses, students need to be drawn into the successful process of conflict resolution communication techniques and strategies.

Students need to feel that someone cares about them, that their perspective and their feelings are heard and validated, and their personal worth and value as individuals is acknowledged. Conflict resolution communication recognizes the student's need to be understood, the parent's right to be heard, the educator's responsibility to enable the student to grow and to become empowered, and the professional's determination to recognize and to commend peaceful negotiation. Unfortunately, providing alternatives to acts of violence in school settings is of paramount importance as weekly news stories and reports of copy-cat tragedies unfold in classrooms, school cafeterias, and on playgrounds. Through interactive participation, the blending of effective communication skills and conflict resolution strategies provides an essential remedy, a real hope, and an effective method of solving conflicts peacefully. *Conflict Resolution Communication: Patterns Promoting Peaceful Schools* offers an efficient and proven strategy for solving problems peacefully and provides an array of lifetime coping skills as a much needed solution to school violence everywhere.

Currently, the crime rate across the United States is declining due to several factors: tougher prison sentences, stricter gun laws, smarter police strategies, stronger police forces, weaker crack epidemic, and a decrease in the number of males who have traditionally been credited with committing a disproportionate number of crimes (*U.S. News & World Report*, January 11, 1999). The Justice Department's National Crime Victimization Survey stated: "Americans suffered less at the hands of criminals in 1997 than since the poll was first taken in 1973, and that a new Justice Department study found that the nation's 1997 murder rate was the lowest in three decades" (*U.S. News & World Report*, 1999, p. 2). With the population of teens on the rise, however, another crime wave may be in the future. Others feel the decrease in crime is temporary. UCLA professor emeritus James Q. Wilson states, "Sure, crime is down, but not compared to thirty-five years ago. We've made gains, but we're not back to the Garden of Eden yet" (*U.S. News & World Report*, 1999, p. 2). Thus, even if crime fluctuates over years and decades, the need for trained conflict resolution communication specialists to lessen situations of violence will remain.

The format of the text encompasses successful strategies, techniques, and processes that bring about effective change in behavior patterns and lead to issue identification, the use of communication practices, and the dissolution of disagreements through conflict resolution communication. Chapter 1: Conflict Resolution Communication Patterns explains how old patterns of behavior can lead to repetitive instances of miscommunication, narrow-mindedness, and an intolerance and indifference for cultural diversity. Worn-out patterns that obstruct change and taking responsibility for one's actions are discussed and explored, and new alternatives available through conflict resolution communication techniques are introduced. Inappropriate acts and violent behaviors affecting interpersonal relationships can be disarmed by reformulating the concepts of compromise, negotiation, and agreement are formulated.

A resolution for diplomatic avenues of accord or harmony is introduced in Chapter 2: Conflict Resolution Communication: A Solution for Peace. By revising old patterns of conceptualizing, processing, and understanding necessary factors for negotiation, cultures can successfully redefine their roles through the interactive process of problem solving, brainstorming, and communication strategies. Intervention of early preventive measures in peer mediation, negotiation, compromise, and decision making will lead to nonviolent behaviors and responsive proposals to peacemaking efforts and conflict resolution communication education.

A wealth of information, including examples and actual procedures for interjecting new patterns of communication and mediation objectives are presented in Chapter 3: Conflict Resolution Communication Strategies. Through situational role-plays, feedback exercises, and interactive improvisations, students learn to control anger and use critical thinking skills before retreating to past behavioral patterns. Differences stemming from cultural, social, economic, and academic levels are perceived from environment and background settings, which require the intervention of thinking, communication, and listening skills. Proactive tools, including the application of communication theory to conflict resolution communication techniques, lead to new patterns of behavior and future directions for the advancement of peaceful negotiation.

A new development in identifying the issues comes from retelling the series of events leading to the participant's involvement in conflict. This approach is introduced in Chapter 4: Narrative Conflict Resolution Communication. Through storytelling, the conflicting parties detach from the emotional side of the altercation and learn to communicate from the point of view of the narrator. By sharing more details in a safe atmosphere, the participants are able to role-play situations and analyze conflict using critical thinking skills to diffuse differences.

Chapter 5: Negotiation: The Opposing Sides of Verbal and Nonverbal Communication depicts the many facets of silent and spoken communication and its power over the negotiation process. Too often, unspoken communication may "speak louder than words" and be misinterpreted or misconstrued and result in conflict. The successful application of verbal and nonverbal cues—body movements, gestures, and facial expressions—leads to effective solutions between dissenting parties.

Miscommunication, rumors, harassments, hearsay, and provocations tend to lead into an area of physical and emotional abuse commonly known as "bullying." Chapter 6: The Brutality of Bullying relates the reasons for and the effects of this terrifying and manipulative behavior leading to fear, intrepidation, and conflict. Healthy coping strategies are introduced and the importance of community involvement in stopping the effects of bullying are described. The internal causes or reasons for the power and the control exhibited by the bully over his or her victim are revealed, understood, and removed through conflict resolution communication practices.

The following three chapters illustrate the role and the importance of conflict resolution strategies for the educator, the parent, and the student. Chapter 7: Conflict Resolution Communication Techniques for Teachers and Administrators provides instructional strategies and disciplinary philosophies to ensure a safe learning environment. By training staff, administrators, and teachers to recognize the early warning signs of distressed individuals, offering impulse-control seminars and anger management skills, and providing conflict resolution communication techniques, professionals can help students reduce school violence and confrontations. Schools must stand behind the victims and encourage them to come forward and engage the entire school community to rally around banning weapons on school grounds and enforcing harsh penalties for perpetrators.

Chapter 8: Conflict Resolution Communication Techniques for Parents guides parents in connecting with their children in ways that improve communication and understanding one another better while restoring a sense of family. Parents serve as examples or role models to their children. When a "disconnect" occurs between parent and child, conflict resolution communication techniques can restore the quality of the familial relationship and the interpersonal messaging and verbal communication necessary to hear, listen, and relate personal viewpoints to one another. Tips offered to parents range from praising and spending positive time with their child to encouraging interactive and ongoing communication to maintain a positive working relationship.

Chapter 9: Conflict Resolution Communication Techniques for Students addresses effective strategies for students to become decision makers, critical thinkers, and problem-solving analysts. They are encouraged to share their thoughts, discuss reasons for their behaviors, identify issues, take time-outs when needed, recognize leadership roles, learn respect and tolerance for others, and develop empathy for recognized differences in others. Students deserve to learn in a healthy environment where they can cooperate in peaceful ways to dispel conflict and apply learning skills for a lifetime.

The final chapter, Chapter 10: Changing Behavior Patterns: The End Is Only the Beginning proclaims the continuous reversal of old worn-out behavior patterns by improved, enhanced, and peaceful ways of dealing with diversity in the future. It is my hope that one day the principles and the applications of conflict resolution communication will reduce violent acts and promote the acceptance and implementation of new behavior patterns that will lead to a lifetime of peace for one and all.

1

Conflict Resolution
Communication Patterns

"Bad habits are like a comfortable bed,
easy to get into, but hard to get out of."
— Anonymous

Patterns are like puzzle pieces. They fall into place securely and without much resistance, forming a connection between today and the rest of our lives. A familiarity or a repetitive pattern frequently gives authority to the formulation of our decisions. Our choices, like the strong weave of a delicate fabric in a particular pattern, may exhibit a steady pull toward a routine "comfort" or "reassurance zone." A sense of stability based on what we know and what we accept contributes to feelings of security in our everyday coping skills.

Educators, parents, and administrators know all too often that the choices made by students in a world of conflict can lack sound judgment and prove to be disastrous. Behavior patterns of younger and less-experienced generations tend to be learned, modeled, or created by influences as early as the preschool years. Patterns are constructed and accepted on a positive or a negative note even before entering school. The problem arises when the behavior patterns reflect denial, hurt, anger, and indifference toward friends, family, and the community itself. These ingrained patterns of comfort or familiarity may deny responsibility for the subsequent consequences, and result in apathy toward those whose lives are changed forever through a lack of control and power maneuvers. Students often act out what they can get away with, and they often want someone to care enough to let them know their own limits.

Being able to choose appropriate options and identify choices helps all of us to make the best decisions for all concerned in a compromising or negotiating manner. A sense of fairness or a "win-win" attitude for dissenting parties diffuses a hostile atmosphere when presented with compassion, empathy, and an acceptance of diversity and under-standing other points of view. Conflict resolution communication provides an effective process for dealing with interpersonal rela-tionships. Successful communication skills depend on listening tech-niques, eye-to-eye contact, gestures, body movements, and the ex-pression of feelings to promote problem solving and reaching an agreement acceptable to all parties. Conflict resolution communication practices can establish a calmer, safer, and more accessible envi-ronment.

Sometimes, however, the threads unravel and expose a "break-away" pattern. We realize quickly that our conduct and actions direct future outcomes. The human spirit, a relatively fragile mechanism, needs support, encouragement, and nurturing to find its way. Direction often comes from prior occurrences or by creating new ones. The comfort of knowing the past and relying on similar outcomes to future experiences creates a sense of well-being. Familiarity provides that comfort and links our behavior to past patterns in order to solve a problem.

Unfortunately, this pattern may not always be the healthiest choice for our continued growth, development, and application of conflict res-olution communication skills. A higher degree of critical thinking skills is necessary for effective negotiation and for blending new and rein-forced habits. The implementation of such a pattern of coping strategies and communication techniques can benefit the remainder of our lives. The strength of a single fiber influences what we do and how we do it, creating successful patterns and diminishing our need for de-structive confrontation.

Our options to choose common lifestyle patterns or to make new choices remain intermingled with previously learned behaviors. Many of us refuse to let go of the comfort or modify the same old patterns. Even as we become older and, hopefully, wiser in applying lifetime so-lutions, we generally stick to our daily habits and simply impose old ways over fresh starts, or implement better ways over threadbare, worn-out routines because of our tendency to hold onto familiar and repetitive patterns. Although comfort may feel informal and allow routine decision-making, change in the form of difficult choices and uneasy responses to new patterns of behavior can lead to improved ways and better habits of dealing with differences in a tolerant and nonviolent manner.

Doing what we know best tends to influence our lives and our relationships significantly. We learn to handle situations in certain ways, often relying on role-model reinforcement or by example. Our parents, siblings, friends, and acquaintances become our role models. Their actions, words, and behaviors have a lasting effect on our abilities to cope with and to apply problem-solving techniques in our daily lives. (See figure 1.1.)

Young people feel enormous amounts of peer pressure as they move through the higher grades. The various ways they look, talk, and feel about relevant issues often carbon-copy the same voice representing the youth culture. Whether students stand together and make a strong impression on the world, whether they actively engage in a rebellious stage, or whether they choose to stand alone and lead in a new or different direction, young people need to feel accepted and recognized. They need to follow or lead others into unchartered territory. Acknowledging that previous generations cycled through similar challenges is not the issue. Rather, young people shape their thoughts, at-

Figure 1.1 Conflict Resolution Communication Role Model Factor

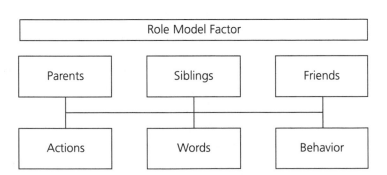

titudes, and concerns by past acceptable actions or through others who offer what they feel may be missing or lacking in their lives.

We reinforce our natural coping skills through observing standards and applying the evidence that supports our realities and our understanding of a situation. Customary patterns of behavior resurface in problem situations because they are familiar, not because they are necessarily correct. Recognizable coping mechanisms bring a sense of comfort and trust to new situations. To deal with a situation is to deal with our past, our culture, our beliefs, and our values. Our impressionable nature becomes molded by static environmental factors and by the evidence and facts we apply to our sense of reality.

Traditionalized Coping Patterns

In other words, we become who we are based on our past relationships and experiences. Those coping strategies and management techniques spill into future situations, and they become "traditionalized" into the efforts we make in negotiation in dealing with third parties. The shape of our natures come up against an unpredictable, uncontrollable, and, of late, a fanatical school environment. Bad habits tend to stagnate and prevent modification of our expectations. Limits can slow growth and development. Resistance to change often stems from miscommunication, lack of information, third-party involvement, "he said/she said" accusations, threats, rumors, and harassing statements. In addition, miscommunication contributes to chaos and confusion within interpersonal relationships and skews our sense of reason.

Too often, people fall into patterns that either enhance their individuality or detract from their unique sense of self. Who they are or what they will become remains unknown to them and others for an extended time or maybe even a total lifespan. Social, cultural, economic, educational, and societal factors influence the makeup of our thought process. What happened yesterday or last week or several years ago affects the way we think, speak, react, and carry out our learned patterns or repetitious behaviors. If we gain rewards, acceptance, or acknowledgment from others by our actions or deeds, then those actions become part of our pattern of being. The patterns in question concern those habits or lifestyle routines that encourage the status quo rather than growth, which drains the energy a person needs at some point to be able to move ahead and make changes.

Conflict Resolution Communication Patterns

Conflict resolution communication affords individuals the opportunity to evaluate their patterns of the past, to recognize choices in their future lifestyles, and to adapt peaceful negotiation strategies and communication techniques for self-improvement, the betterment of others, and those of society. It encourages strength of character in every individual, an understanding of human differences to diffuse conflict, and a realization that new or untried coping skills may become the core of life-long learning. By learning to listen to others, hearing the message being conveyed, appreciating various points of view, and isolating the issues at hand, individuals can more effectively adjust to routine or everyday situations, using a higher level of understanding, tolerance, and critical thinking.

Rather than remain in set behavior patterns that inhibit personal growth, inspire manipulation, and encourage loss of control and self-esteem, individuals need to find their level of comfort that promotes the worth of self in relation to family, friends, and society. They need to build strong communication skills and coping strategies for a peaceful and healthier future. By understanding the influences of the past on their behavior patterns, they can identify those patterns that need to be strengthened, preserved, or changed in a world of rich diversity and opportunity.

Too often, within the school environment, young minds blend into "paper-doll" people and become unrecognizable figures of one voice, whether wearing designer jeans or displaying colored locks or tiers of body piercing. Gangs, cliques, and swarms of impressionable youth wait for further directions, mimicking the latest thinking patterns and the most desirable actions. Coping skills or dealing with differences becomes, in a sense, intolerable to those seeking peer approval or choosing to reject negotiations instead of finding an appropriate way to solve disputes without violence. Fighting, bullying, or teasing become ingrained patterns or ways of "saving face" without losing power, control, and identity recognition. To avoid looking small or less important to peers, some individuals mimic or parrot their generation's cultural message, actions, and mindset to the point of intolerance and indifference. Using threats or harassments to pressure others or to control situations of status and power often results in fear and inappropriate acts of violence, which will not be tolerated in any school system throughout the country. Engaging in unacceptable or improper behaviors in social settings becomes an unfortunate pattern for many cliques that value the feeling of belonging to a peer group over choosing acceptable conduct that promotes tolerance, caring, and a healthy respect for differences. Withdrawing that clenched fist, biting back those angry words, and refraining from painful accusations and put downs are not acts of weakness but, rather, a choice of strength not enough students choose when faced with diversity in schools. However, the choice to fight, to conceal weapons in bookbags and jackets, to wear headgear or arm bands signifying gang involvement, or to push someone beyond their limit causing them to hurt others seems to be the unfortunate first choice of many when responding to situations that stem from differences.

Consider the alarming findings in school crime rates as reported in 1993 by the National Education Association (*Time*, January 25, 1993, p. 1):

- 100,000 students took guns to schools.
- 160,000 secondary students skipped classes because they feared physical harm.
- 40 students were hurt or killed by firearms.
- 260 students were physically assaulted.
- 6,250 teachers were threatened with bodily injury or harm.

The National Center for Injury Prevention and Control, and the Statistical Abstract text of the United States reported in 1999 that between 1994 and 1998 that (1) 173 violent deaths occurred in schools across the nation; (2) 50 percent of children ages 9 to 17 were worried about dying young; and (3) 31 percent of children ages 12 to 17 knew someone their age who carried a gun (*Time*, 1999, p. 1). These alarming results send a message that changing the behaviors and patterns of conduct in youth requires them to embrace cultural differences in a safe, motivating, and inspirational learning environment infused with conflict resolution communication practices.

Whether it's a nine-year-old girl who chooses to carry her father's loaded gun to school in Pennsylvania because she feels threatened or bullied by another student or whether it's a young man who returns to school with a loaded revolver to settle a fight on the playground in Louisiana, all students must accept responsibility for their options and abide by schools' enforcement of a "zero tolerance" policy for violence that results in immediate suspensions or expulsions. The right choices need to be made by students to prevent school violence and promote alternative practices for negotiation and resolution of differences. Patterns of behavior need to be restructured and refocused on building peace within classrooms, in the school cafeterias, in the hallways, in the locker rooms, and on and off school grounds.

In trying to remain within their "comfort zone," many people rely heavily on familiar patterns and behaviors. We try to use what we know, what seems familiar, and what brought about or produced sudden results or temporary solutions. By not isolating or identifying the issues, the problems, or the mistakes of the past, our coping skills become clouded with doubts and burdened by unnecessary baggage. The inability to deal openly and carefully with current problems leaves us vulnerable to repeating the same patterns of the past, twisting and struggling to fit the old pieces into the present puzzle. The resistance to change and to new ways to scrutinize, analyze, and evaluate situations is the mark of a tired and worn perspective. Reliance on accusations, harassing comments, and threats to make others acquiesce creates violence and inappropriate behavior. Problem-solving techniques and effective resolutions get lost in unrelated issues and uncertainty. Without clear identification of issues, information, and alternative sources to resolve conflicts, we must play out the same old patterns of the past and endure the same effects of those decisions determined by the lack of communication skills.

Our denial only hampers the ability to redefine and refocus on new ways of handling conflicts and facilitating effective solutions to real problems. By breaking the destructive patterns of the past and eliminating the climate of manipulation, fear, and the formidable pressure of status and hierarchy control, we learn to create an atmosphere of sound judgment, receptiveness, and strengthening change. Being willing to consciously extend beyond boundaries of the past into a reasonable and rationale future relationship demonstrates a decision to create new patterns for growth and necessary change.

An opportunity for continued expansion and transformation occurs when we feel most uncomfortable with our behavior patterns. The challenge of regaining control of who we are and what we are all about represents a dynamic trend toward self-empowerment and valued perspectives. When we no longer need a safety net or a "crutch" to support our old habits and repetitive patterns, we learn to rely on our own sense of determination and empowerment. Our need to recognize, to explore, and to accumulate new behavior patterns will be a natural part of future decisions, actions, and thought patterns. That awareness of alternative processes for solving situations, altercations, and violence sheds new light on differences and what divides us. Skills, strategies, and critical reasoning techniques introduced in conflict resolution communication become the norm for handling problems. We develop a sense of just and fair play that elevates our conscious choices, enabling us to solve problems in a "win-win" manner through compromise, negotiation, and a sense of mutual respect.

As our ability to understand the reasons of our actions expands and a sense of enlightenment clarifies meaning, our critical thought process becomes sharper helping us ascertain suitable new or different behavior patterns. The transformation is not simple, and may tax our efforts to change course and to move into an appealing line of compromise for all concerned. However, the effects of our new behaviors are certain to lead to stable growth and a newfound confidence based on a fresh sense of self-awareness, self-esteem, and a desire to make better choices in stressful situations.

The challenges of getting along with other people, compromising, negotiating, and problem-solving solutions are not a cliché, but these behaviors are the core of the conflict resolution process and of effective communication skills. Conflict resolution communication strategies fulfill the needs of communities throughout the nation by providing formidable alternatives to litigation. The advancement and promotion of peaceful solutions through effective coping strategies, listening skills, and mediation teaching techniques will become the mainstay for understanding the origin and the resolution of conflict. The conflict resolution communication specialist can help communities, students, parents, employers, employees, educators, and those in need of alternative mediation services handle conflicts constructively and appropriately, without violence, while mastering life-long communication skills. Mediation services in the areas of family dispute, divorce, parenting, business, government, education, and community policing will be more operative and accessible. Through conflict resolution skills, communities can better understand and resolve differences during the fluctuations of change and growth.

Cultural attitudes profoundly influence individual attitudes toward violence. Is violence perceived as exciting and stimulating? Do we express cynicism or hopefulness about our ability to solve problems such as racism, sexism, and the role of the media in shaping the values of the existing culture? Is the approved or recommended way to resolve conflicts through the use of violence? The interdependence of the actions, thoughts, and behavior patterns of the individual, the family, the school, the workplace, and the community affects the nature of conflict (Fried & Fried, 1996, p. 9). The acceptance of situations invested in cultural and social diversity leads to greater tolerance and harmony throughout the nation. Professionally trained conflict resolution communication specialists can help advance peaceful solutions through effective coping strategies, listening skills, and mediation teaching techniques, which provide a foundation for understanding the origin and the resolution of conflict. (See figure 1.2.)

The field of conflict resolution reaches into every aspect of human development and interpersonal relationships. Social interaction in the home, in the workforce, and in communities can be greatly affected by the conflict resolution communication program. By providing effective communication and conflict resolution skills needed to diffuse violent altercations and acknowledge differences, individuals will be able to isolate conflicting issues, understand communication patterns, and work together to resolve differences.

Figure 1.2 Conflict Resolution Communication Specialist

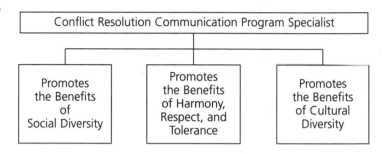

2

Conflict Resolution Communication: A Solution for Peace

"Elegance of language may not be in the power of all of us; but simplicity and straightforwardness are. Write much as you would speak; speak as you think. Be what you say; and, within the rules of prudence, say what you are."
— Alford

Violence in schools, random shootings, acts of intimidation, and senseless hate crimes are unnecessary and inappropriate patterns of behavior. Abusive and controlling actions demonstrate thoughtlessness, indifference, intolerance, and a lack of respect for others. The core of the problem is to find out and reveal the reasons for such acts and then to treat this type of meaningless behavior with effective intervention skills using conflict resolution and communication strategies. In responding to volatile situations, intermediaries can present ways to effectively cool down heated conflicts and find solutions using compromise and negotiation techniques. Whether episodes of youth violence or incidents of rage against society, disputes of any nature must be resolved in a nonviolent manner. Conflict resolution communication strategies and effective mediation skills play a critical role in downplaying prominent differences between parties and in clarifying relevant issues. The lack of control and sound judgment in heated circumstances is never an easy situation to rectify. A great deal of honest hard work and sincere efforts is required in finding answers to situations of conflict.

Mediation conferences and workshops throughout the United States bring together skilled negotiators, educators, social workers, legal experts, community activists, and students in an effort to find effective and meaningful ways to resolve disputes in a nonviolent manner. New tools for retraining processes of listening, paraphrasing, problem solving, brainstorming, and communicating lessen repetitive patterns of learned behavior in dealing with conflict. Students and peer mediators from public and private schools learn mediation techniques through early intervention programs to help them adopt effective methods of negotiation and compromising solutions. Continued use and implementation of anger management skills and strategies for dealing with difficult situations strengthens nonviolent and successful coping abilities. Improved social interactions, family dynamics, relationships, community and school-related activities, learning environments, vocational training, and life-long experiences are just a few of the benefits of effective application of mediated resolution strategies and effective communication skills.

The dynamics of the conflict resolution process include a clear understanding of the mediation procedure, its benefits, and how it compares to other forms of negotiating solutions and resolving conflicts. A concise description of the situation by each party to the dispute, given from his or her particular viewpoint is needed. The next step uses effective communication to identify issues, needs, and wants in helping the parties to determine a mediated resolution.

Brainstorming or problem solving by the respondents is a recognized approach and encouraged by the facilitator. Both parties use compromise and negotiation methods to explore and refine a mutually acceptable mediation agreement in written contract form that specifies acceptable resolutions. As adults and youth acquire and implement effective mediation strategies, a working relationship or a team partnership takes place in resolving issues. Additional time and discussions allow the mediation team to decide how it will function, be managed, and who will take on specific negotiation roles. Routine efforts to keep the mediation team on track also help alert it to any unintended issues that need to be resolved. The power balance among youth and adult mediators can be shared jointly by alternating the mediator role. Modeling the balance of adult and youth roles in mediation through role-plays, discussions, and extemporaneous simulations builds a viable partnership in an atmosphere of cooperation.

Individuals able to isolate conflicting issues and understand communication patterns generally work together more effectively to resolve differences. Research studies in conflict resolution and mediation practices suggest countless approaches to help reduce violence and move toward a more peaceful society. (See figure 2.1.)

Prior to the start of the mediation process, a handout on the do's and don'ts of mediation should be distributed to all disputants. The mediation rules involve careful listening skills, fairness guidelines, confidentiality procedures, voluntary agreement to mediate, a genuine respect for others' thoughts by the individuals, and a personal account from the disputants of the issues that need to be addressed. The mediators must remember to remain neutral and not take sides or show a personal bias toward the issues, answer questions for the respondents, or tell them what to do. Casting blame for the situation, giving advice, or looking for witnesses to corroborate conflicting events should never occur during mediated sessions.

Negotiating at Impartial Tables

For an effective balance of power during the mediation process, eye contact, acknowledgment of the issues, listening style, and response to the feelings and behavior of the respondents must be effectual and without compromise. A response by the mediator to the validation of

Figure 2.1 Conflict Resolution Communication Model

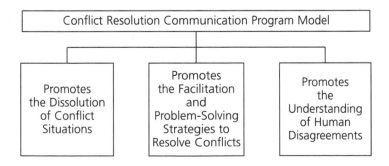

the feelings of the disputant or students should be made and noted without condescension. If strong emotions or the fear of retaliation by either party prevails throughout the mediating session, then a caucus or a time-out session needs to be enforced. A follow-up or a post-mediation session is advisable to ask whether the mediation agreement is working in resolving the issues. Unfortunately, many difficult situations arise in mediation sessions and must be dealt with by using effective communication strategies. The trained mediator, using his or her skills and expertise, focuses the process on relevant issues and significant needs. Helping parties to frame issues centered around fairness, recognition, safety, identity, belonging, and empathy emphasizes the motivation and reasoning for conflict, rather than stresses the differences and hostilities that lead to continuous problems. An agreement to actively participate in the mediation process, to follow the rules in a cooperative manner, to show respect for the other person's right to communicate verbally, and to commit to careful listening and negotiating standards sets the tone for effective conflict resolution processes.

Listening and communication skills are needed to diffuse conflicts, resolve situations without violence, and create a paradigm shift in the identification and understanding of human disagreements. Cultural differences, misunderstandings, lack of information, rumors, and hearsay too often lead to the breakdown of positive communication, tolerance and respect for humanity, and peaceful negotiation. Through the implementation of problem-solving techniques and mediation strategies on a long-term basis, dealing with altercations and difficult situations becomes second nature to future generations.

The field of conflict resolution reaches into every aspect of human development and interpersonal relationships. Social interaction taking place in the home, in the workforce, and in communities can be greatly affected through conflict resolution education by providing effective communication and conflict resolution skills.

Unfortunately, conflict is rarely acted upon as an opportunity to learn and to grow emotionally and intellectually before the altercation develops into violence and acts of tragedy. Opportunity to make things better comes before events get out of hand. Conflict resolution education provides students a rare opportunity to diffuse differences and shift to a new paradigm of thought by stepping into another person's perspective to handle conflicts productively. Violence will always be a regrettable part of society, which emphasizes the need to handle conflicts constructively for maximum benefit to all parties. (See figure 2.2.)

Conflict resolution education supports violence prevention policies by helping students accept the consequences of their own behavior and by developing personal and responsible behavior management skills and workable processes for solving problems before they escalate to violence. A conflict resolution education program models, teaches, and incorporates the techniques and problem-solving skills of mediation, negotiation, and collaboration. Students trained in conflict resolution techniques readily apply their skills to situations in and out of school more constructively. "Eighty-five percent adopt negotiation as their primary approach to conflict, rather than use threats or violence" (Conflict Resolution Education Network, 2000, p. 2). Negative attitudes and behaviors displayed by students visibly diminish due to participation in mediation training. Conflict resolution education also affects the overall dynamics of individual growth and positive interaction in the following ways (CREnet, 2000):

Law-Related Education
• Helps students understand the relationship between law, rights, and personal and community responsibility.

Figure 2.2 Conflict Resolution Communication

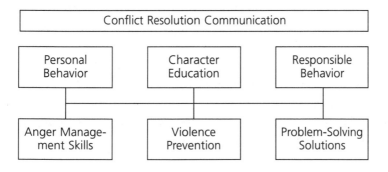

Social and Emotional Skill Development
- Helps students develop anger management skills.
- Helps students incorporate personal relationship-building skills.
- Helps students develop fundamental competencies (self-control, self-respect, empathy, teamwork) needed to make a successful transition into adulthood.

Improved Intergroup Relations
- Teaches the principles and skills needed to respect others as individuals and group members.
- Teaches responsible and productive intergroup relations.

Improved Academic Performance
- Builds cognitive skills.
- Builds confidence.

Responsible Citizenship
- Models the expression of concerns and interests in a peaceful and productive way.
- Provides the ability to solve problems for the mutual benefit of community members.

The benefits of conflict resolution education within the community will be evidenced in the lasting effects and life-long skills of problem-solving and peacemaking strategies developed and implemented by mediators and students. Collaboration among educators, mental health professionals, parents, students, and community groups and organizations is also critical in creating schools that work to protect students in a safe learning environment.

Conflict resolution education provides society with an effective and useful tool to solve conflicts peacefully by using communication skills, mediation strategies, and negotiation processes. The ultimate goal is to implement school-wide education and training to maintain a safe school learning environment and provide effective coping strategies for individual violence prevention. Creating a climate of tolerance dissipates violence as future generations learn alternative methods to deal with differences and provides numerous benefits, including the following (U.S. Dept. of Education and Justice, 2000):

- Resolve problems and disputes nonviolently.
- Refrain from bullying.
- Show respect.
- Report crimes and threats of violence to officials.
- Get involved in the development and implementation of anticrime programs.
- Learn how to avoid becoming a victim.
- Seek help from trusted adults when confronting difficult problems.

Being treated with respect and being treated equally, regardless of ethnicity, race, religion, sex, socioeconomic status, or other characteristics reinforces a new paradigm of harmonious and diplomatic relationships among all people.

Conflict resolution education grew out of the social justice concerns of the 1960s. Just as the Quakers had incorporated peacemaking and problem solving into their teachings, religious and peace activists groups adopted this cause in the late 1970s and integrated dispute resolution into their educational curriculums (CREnet, 2000). Community mediation centers focused on interpersonal and neighborhood conflicts while schools incorporated law-related educational projects into their course of study.

The National Association for Mediation in Education (NAME) was formed at the University of Massachusetts at Amherst in 1984 by a group of educators, activists, and community mediators in the field of conflict resolution education. Their purpose was to act as a support network and materials clearinghouse for conflict resolution in schools. NAME merged in 1995 with the National Institute for Dispute Resolution (NIDR) and became the Conflict Resolution Education Network (CREnet) at the NIDR. It serves today as the primary national and international clearinghouse for information, resources, and technical assistance in the field of conflict resolution and education. It also promotes the development, implementation, and institutionalization of school and university-based conflict resolution programs and curriculum. "In 1997, there were over 8,500 school-based conflict resolution programs in the United States, located in the nation's 86,000 public schools" (CREnet, 2000, p.1).

Conflict Resolution Communication Education

Conflict resolution education promotes an environment rich in diversity and tolerant of genders, social class, physical and mental abilities, and sexual orientation. By creating a safe environment mindful of all human beings, the process and practice of conflict resolution education fills an ongoing need for acceptance and awareness of cultural differences and individual strengths. Relationships of inequality and power, prejudice and discrimination, and cultural and social differences are challenged by new ways of communicating and understanding (Bodine & Crawford, 1998).

A commitment to study conflict constructively and find appropriate and acceptable ways to deal with differences peacefully fosters the goal of learning in a sound environment of social justice and equality. The implementation of a conflict resolution education enables communities to offer the skills and knowledge necessary to successfully nurture an environment rich in diversity, to accept inevitable conflicts from differing values, to understand that conflict presents an opportunity for growth, self-awareness, and a respect for others, and that this articulated vision can enrich and strengthen school and workplace communities (Bodine & Crawford, 1998).

Conflict resolution education not only presents sound principles of effectively dealing with various forms of violence, but it provides communication and listening skills to handle the issues in relationships. Communication consists of the expressive skill of speaking and the receptive skill of listening. Active listening techniques include the effective use of eye contact, head nodding, gestures, and body positioning to promote communication between all parties. Successful communication conveys the speaker's intention and the confirms the listener's response. A cooperative learning environment improves the climate in schools and communities while challenging young people to see peaceful and interactive communities as a realistic goal in today's society. Necessary environmental conditions may include increasing levels of respect, trust, cohesiveness, caring, morale, and opportunities for academic and social growth and community and school renewal (Bodine & Crawford, 1998).

Negotiation, mediation, and decision making serve as effective dispute resolution models that provide nonadversarial and nonviolent methods to litigation, discipline policies at schools, and referral processes at work. Conflict resolution education builds on cooperative and collaborative principles of learning from controversies, turning conflicts into opportunities to manifest new viewpoints of understanding, developing self-control and efforts of self-discipline, and accepting responsibility for personal choices, actions, and follow-up consequences (Bodine & Crawford, 1998).

The following sound precepts or principles of conflict resolution education exist within a cooperative learning environment (Bodine & Crawford, 1998, p. 47):

- Conflict is natural and normal.
- Differences can be acknowledged and appreciated.
- Conflict viewed as a solution-building opportunity can lead to positive change.
- When the conflicting parties build on one another's strengths to find solutions, they create a climate that nurtures individual self-worth and fulfills individuals' needs.

Conflict resolution education proactively addresses the skills, strategies, and an understanding of the mediation process that promote safe environments and generations of responsible adults. Providing alternative forms of compromise and negotiation techniques reduces self-destruction and violent acts of behavior by working through conflicts involving intrapersonal, interpersonal, and intergroup situations (Bodine & Crawford, 1998).

Conflict is a natural, vital part of life. When conflict is understood, it can become an opportunity to learn and create. The challenge for people in conflict is to apply the principles of creative cooperation in their human relationships. (Bodine, Crawford & Schrumph, 1994, p. xxiii)

In a country where guns claim some 30,000 lives a year, school shootings contribute to concern and fear about the availability of weapons (Reuters, May 26, 2000). A 1998 Gallup poll cited the fear of crime and violence as the most frequent response mentioned by 20 percent of Americans to this most important noneconomic problem question: "What do you think is the most important problem facing this country today?" (Gallup, 1998, p. 61). Hundreds of thousands of protestors attended the "Million Mom March" in May 2000 in Washington, and rallied to demand that Congress pass what they called "common sense gun control" measures to stem the violence. The National Association of Attorneys General recorded at least 14 U.S. school shooting incidents that claimed casualties in the past seven years, including multiple killings in Oregon, Arkansas, and Kentucky. Excluded from these incidents was the worst tragedy in the series of school shootings in April 1999 at Littleton, Colorado, when two students rampaged through Columbine High School, killing 13 people before taking their own lives (Reuters, 2000).

Though often used as a reactive tool to violent incidents, conflict resolution education works best as an integral part of violence prevention. By constructively addressing issues of conflict that often proceed physical encounters, the incidence and intensity of physical engagement diminish (Bodine & Crawford, 1998). Teamwork among educators, mental health professionals, parents, students, and community groups and organizations is also critical in creating schools that work to keep students safe and better protected in the school environment. Secretary of Education Richard W. Riley stated in an address to a school guidance counselor's meeting in Chicago:

We cannot rely on mechanical profiling of students. We simply cannot put student behaviors into a formula to come up with the appropriate response. We need human involvement—your professional judgment—in every step of the process. I'd like to challenge school counselors to lead the effort to ensure that as schools work to keep

students safe, we avoid overreacting and stereotyping. With your help,
we can keep the focus on building strong connections between teachers,
parents, and student." (Department of Education, April 28, 2000, p. 1)

Schools and communities are encouraged to develop a comprehensive team approach to violence prevention as addressed in *Safeguarding Our Children: An Action Guide*, written by the Departments of Education (ED) and Justice (DOJ). The guide recommends the following interventions (U.S. Dept. of Education, 2000, p. 2):

1. Create a school-wide foundation that fosters positive discipline, academic success, and mental and emotional wellness.
2. Intervene early with the 10–15 percent of students at risk for severe academic or behavioral problems.
3. Provide immediate and intensive mediation for students who continue to experience significant emotional and behavior problems.
4. Improve the school's violence prevention programs and student learning.

Psychological violence, including verbal abuse and nonphysical acts of violence, may be more pervasive than physical forms of violence. These victims are not always recognized as victims because their scars are not physical, but rather emotional. (See figure 2.3.) Whether teased, taunted, harassed, or bullied, victims as well as their tormentors need the benefits of conflict resolution education. By learning to address fear, discrimination, manipulation, and intimidation with effective coping strategies and communication skills, individuals armed with defense and proactive tools can lessen acts of violence and their effects.

To continue focusing on the occurrence of violence is to treat a symptom, offering little for the future. Focus on alternatives to violence offers hope that those alternatives will become the behaviors of choice. The goal of conflict resolution education is to change the environment, creating safe communities in a nonviolent and multicultural society (Bodine & Crawford, 1998). Long-term changes in attitudes and behaviors constitute effective alternatives provided by conflict resolution practices.

Figure 2.3 The Cycle of Violence

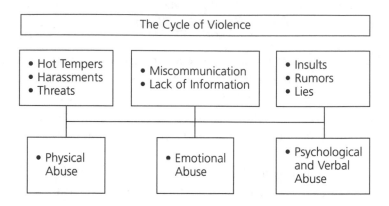

Conflict resolution education offers a theoretical understanding and the practical experience needed to help produce effective, balanced, and flexible adults who use life-long mediation skills and practice alternative methods to reduce violence. The key is trained individuals who can help people learn these skills by leading programs in schools, churches, community organizations, and public agencies.

Designing and implementing a school-based conflict mediation program require clear objectives and goals. To expand the number of nonviolent negotiations and peaceful solutions, students need to be trained as peer mediators and to participate in guided sessions where they are exposed to valuable perspectives and varied points of view. An awareness of the need for mediation needs to dominate educational systems and be embraced through assemblies, speakers, workshops, in-class discussions, journal writings, and role-playing conflict resolution simulations. Students meet with trained conflict counselors and mediators who attentively counsel disruptive and suspended students, as well as connect with quiet, loner-type students and students new to the school system. Community service programs, steering committees consisting of faculty and community members, and active participation of administrators, parents, and students, alike, all contribute to the development mediation.

Conflict resolution communication theory and practice represent a major turning point in alternative approaches to violence in the workplace, in the home, in the school, and in the community. Disputes often take place whenever interaction occurs between individuals or groups of people. Attention needs to focus on using coping strategies, applying effective communication skills in both expressive speaking and receptive listening, identifying the issues, and exploring peaceful ways to bring about solutions and compromise to conflict. Advanced training in conflict resolution education and communication programs serve the public well in dealing with actual problem-solving situations.

For communication theory and principles to affect on the practices of conflict resolution education, effective speaking and active listening skills must be in place to connect conflicting parties that are attempting to reach a solution. Messages and ideas presented by the mediator or the disputants must first be thoroughly understood in context and re-phrased with exact meaning. Direct eye contact and positive body language help to focus on the other person's message. Additional infor-mation through open-ended questions clarifies of the issues directly re-lating to the conflict. Relying on speaking skills for understanding rather than for debate lessens the chance to demean or manipulate the other party. It also advances the listening process and brings the parties closer to the core of the problem. First, the mediator needs to help separate the emotions and hurt feelings from the issues. Then the parties retell the events leading up to the situation. Communication becomes a narrative event for the participants. As a revelation to the speaker and to the audience, a story of actual events releases feelings of blame and guilt based on cultural diversity and individual background experiences. The listener uses a more objective approach in assessing and framing the other person's message and understanding of what led up to the confrontation. The disputants acknowledge the perception of different viewpoints as they clarify the other person's account of the in-cident. Communication is made as simple as possible for all parties to hear and comprehend through the process of conflict resolution.

Conflict resolution education models, teaches, and incorporates the processes and problem-solving skills of mediation, negotiation, and collaboration. Helping disputing parties to solve the problems themselves, using the guidance of the neutral third party, illustrates the basic format of conflict resolution practices. In order to achieve successful collaboration, students must be skilled in listening, reasoning, analytical thinking, reframing, empathizing, probing for more information, summarizing, and grounding the dispute. Their creativity in finding solutions or options comes out of being able to step into another's point of view with a sense of understanding, tolerance, and balance.

Unfortunately, the need for effective conflict resolution and mediation techniques will continue to play a prominent role in our society throughout the twenty-first century. Copycat acts of random violence against society need to be identified and diffused through peaceful means of compromise and negotiation. The implementation of "win-win" solutions must reflect the goal of the mediation process in a workable and nonaggressive manner. Through learning and conflict resolution education, a new level of successful communication can be attained through non-violent behavior and peaceful solutions.

3

Conflict Resolution Communication Strategies

"Seal up the mouth of outrage for a while,
Till we can hear these ambiguities,
And know their spring, their head, their true descent.
And then will I be general of your woes
And lead you, even to death. Meantime forbear,
And let mischance be slave to patience,
Bring forth the parties of suspicion. . . ."
— William Shakespeare, *Romeo and Juliet*

Students have a natural ability and a willingness to demonstrate what they learn and understand. Through interaction and direct involvement in situational role-plays involving differences, conflicts, or miscommunications, young minds widen the strategies they can use to resolve issues. They are hungry for the answers to daily dilemmas and eager to be a part of the solution. They need to be presented with workable remedies that prove relevant, effective, and acceptable, especially for altercations that are characterized by elevating tempers, exploding voices, and aggressive behavior. Young people have the ability to follow the strategies of conflict resolution communication successfully and maintain peaceful resolve while sifting through the issues. Differences, whether cultural, social, academic, or personal, need to be isolated and examined for the cause or the root of the problem by professionals trained in conflict resolution communication strategies.

Participants involved in conflict, no matter what their age, must confirm the issues that are spinning out of control. By working one-on-

one with an experienced mediator or educator trained in conflict resolution procedures, students will be cauched to move heated emotions
aside and examine the reasons for their conflict. Third-party involvement, rumors, lack of information, and miscommunications all
contribute to greater uncertainty. These factors must be laid aside to
isolate the problems at hand. Many disputes are overheated emotions,
hurt feelings, and attempts to " save face" with peers while maintaining
some sense of control, and students tend to argue rather than listening
while the conflict escalates until it takes on a life of its own. Without re-
alizing the very issues that pushed the confrontation into a brouhaha or
a state of confusion in the first place, many students fight to the end in
an effort to regain control or their status or position among their peers.

Too often, altercations among groups of friends, males or females, or
between cultural groups erupt into violence and elicit the dreaded suspensions or expulsions from school grounds. Either knowing one
another for years or not knowing one another at all become minor
factors when emotions boil over and anger turns into violence. Just
looking at one another the wrong way, or reading biased meanings into
blameless eye contact, or bumping shoulders in a crowded corridor, or
not favoring the cultural dress or the color of one's origin become con-
venient excuses for inappropriate comments or misconduct on school
grounds. Students, unfortunately, look for a variety of ways to express
pent-up emotions or angered feelings that may have sprung from
their home environments, backgrounds, or cultural settings. Misunderstandings with a teacher over a grade or an assignment, outside
pressures on the job, or ongoing disagreements with friends or family
members may originate from previous unsettled differences. The
starting point of the conflict is often as baffling to those participants as
it is to administrators and teachers who step in to avert the violence.

Strategic Benefits

Exploring the reasons for conflict and identifying the issues leading to
the first harsh words or to the first act of physical abuse are most ben-
eficial when students feel empowered to make choices and understand

they will be held accountable for their actions. The strategies of conflict resolution communication enable students to think before they act, to listen before they commit to narrow-mindedness, and to choose options that benefit all parties concerned and enable them to find a resolution in a peaceful environment. Through voluntary agreement to mediate and a willingness to communicate in a safe school setting, students learn to apply active listening skills, including direct eye contact, head nodding, and positive body positioning. By not interrupting the mediator or the other parties' description of the incident, student participants learn to listen for details of the incident and to appreciate another point of view before expressing their side of the story. Feedback can take the form of repetitive mirror exercises, of movements of the parties, or of hearing exercises such as answering questions or prompts simultaneously and repeating the exchange. Generally, the results of the verbal and nonverbal messages between the disputants can elicit relief of tension and allow each side to accept a more open and more tolerant assessment of the situation and the reasons leading to the initial confrontation. The effective blending of communication strategies and mediation techniques facilitated by a conflict resolution communication specialist dispels the negativity surrounding the situation quickly and enables the parties to move toward a workable win-win solution.

Finger pointing and blaming the other party for starting the dispute, escalating the anger, inviting third-party involvement, or inflicting the first blow does not dissolve the incident or minimize the pain felt by students involved in the incident. The situation does, however, plead for alternate ways to deal with differences in a peaceful school setting. These methods offer opportunities for growth and new patterns or coping strategies. By learning to control anger and analyze, understand, identify, and communicate thoughts, actions, and needs, these young people can dispel the fear of attending school, being hurt, and witnessing or being part of the violence that permeates learning environments today.

It is imperative that the speaker's intention and the listener's response in conflict resolution communication are conveyed to one another and confirmed through active listening techniques. The mediation session addresses intimidation, manipulation, discrimination, and fear of reprisal with a number of proactive tools. (See figure 3.1.) Further, the security or safety felt within conflict resolution needs to be shared by all participants and favor innovative approaches, frank discussions, nonjudgmental attitudes, tolerance, and progressiveness toward finding better solutions and better choices. Behaviors of choice need to be introduced to students as a basic approach to solving dilemmas and stifling prejudices.

Communication Theory

Communication theory and conflict resolution practices connect conflicting parties attempting to reach a solution. Depending on backgrounds, experience, culture, and understanding of the participants, successful communication may be blocked by a number of variables, including the following (Bodine & Crawford, 1998):

1. People may not be talking to each other.
2. People may not be hearing each other.
3. People misunderstand or misinterpret what is communicated.

The relationship between sound communication theory and its affect on individuals depends their motivation patterns in solving conflicts

Figure 3.1 Proactive Tools for Conflict Resolution Communication

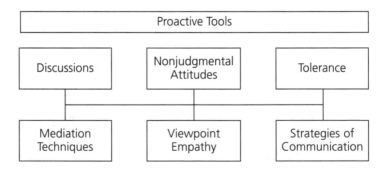

peacefully to the benefit of all parties through the conflict resolution communication program. The integration of theory and the practice of making pertinent choices to negotiate workable solutions to conflict results from understanding and applying the processes. Concrete and realistic examples of theory help students to acquire a thoughtful understanding of theory in the many different contexts of their lives. As they become more systematic, thoughtful, and critical thinkers, students should also be able to identify the persuasiveness element of theory in everyday activities. As they recognize the interdisciplinary nature of theory, they can apply it in real-life situations.

Communication theory, for example, touches on other fields, including psychology, social psychology, sociology, biology, and philosophy. The connection between intrapersonal or knowing oneself, interpersonal, and cross-cultural communication provides relevance to theory (West & Turner, 2000, p. iii).

Rather than remain distant, abstract, and obscure, a "good theory" offers a practical integration of material for students of different ages, socioeconomic and cultural backgrounds, ethnicity, and linguistic variations. Students can acquire useful knowledge and perspectives from simple, understandable, and straightforward theories. Good theories break through the stereotypical notions of scholarship and research by showing the application of communication to many different personal theories daily. By revising their misconceptions of research and theory, students become better critical thinkers and learners (West & Turner, p. iii). A good theory is used to influence programmatic decisions, make research useful, and contribute to productivity or efficiency (Cohen & Brawer, 1989, p. 367).

A good theory provides continuity for students to learn by applying relevancy to real-life instruction through accessibility and flexibility, and presents a consistent pattern of theory demonstrating narrative experiences, assumptions, core concepts, and testable evaluations (West & Turner, p. iv). Theory and theoretical principles integrated into research studies expose students to research content and provide continuity and a balanced presentation of both theory and research (p. v). Communication theorist, John Dewey, focused on the elements of social theory and emphasized the role of communication to life and social interactions. The symbolic interaction theory suggests that individuals construct meaning through the communication process, which offers meaning for human behavior (p. 77). The meaning of theory rests on communication concepts, social reality, and perception. When two people attempt to make sense of the message sequence in their conversation, they either achieve some degree of coordination in their transmitted message or fail to communicate.

Repetitive patterns or rules determine how individuals process information and then choose between alternative behavior patterns in different situations. *Constitutive* rules describe how rules should be interpreted within a given context while helping individuals assign meaning to shared or interactive communication. *Regulative rules* provide guidelines for social behavior by communicating what happens next in a conversation. However, unwanted repetitive patterns of interpersonal communication present sequential and recurring conflicting episodes that are generally unacceptable to participants in a conflict because they follow a structure that obligates them to perform specific behaviors, regardless of the consequences (p. 98). The eventual goal is for more people and groups to be influenced by cultural and social processes—as in conflict resolution communication—that are successfully worked out and implemented through social interaction, tolerance, and acceptance of differences. (See figure 3.2.)

The conflict resolution communication program models, teaches, and incorporates the processes and problem-solving skills of mediation, negotiation, and collaboration.

Figure 3.2 The Processes of Conflict Resolution Communication

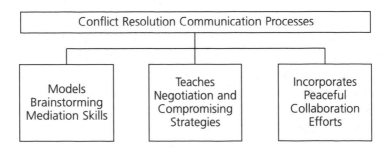

The benefits of conflict resolution education include the following (*School Safety*, 2000, p. 2):

- Support for violence prevention policies by teaching skills and processes to solve problems before they escalate to violence.
- Help for students to develop personal behavioral management skills to act responsibly in the school community and to accept the consequences of their own behavior.
- Help for students to develop the fundamental competencies of self-control, self-respect, empathy, and teamwork.
- Help for students to make a successful transition to adulthood.
- Develop cognitive skills for students necessary for high academic achievement.
- Teach students to respect others as individuals and as group members.
- Teach students how to build and maintain responsible and productive intergroup relations.

We are the living product of our environment, our culture, and the personal evidence that we collect to mold our very existence. Our parents, siblings, friends, and acquaintances become our role models. Their actions, words, and behaviors produce a lasting effect on our abilities to cope with and to apply problem-solving techniques to personal differences in our daily lives. Hearing the other side of the story and listening to what the other person has to say represent two processes that need to be mastered and applied to negotiations.

4

Narrative
Communication

*"If you do not tell the truth about yourself you
cannot tell it about other people."*
— Virginia Woolf

Through dialogue, storytelling, and narrative mediation techniques, the parties involved in altercations and repeated conflicts can find effective means of resolving feelings of guilt, power, and blame. Conflicting parties focus on what is being conveyed and their reactions to various points of view. A new understanding of the issues emerges without the bitter resentment, hatred, and combativeness associated with repeated conflicts and syndromes of violence. Students tend to show remarkable success with narrative mediation or telling their side of the story through the role of an observer or another participant involved in the conflict. Through calibrated degrees of separation, students move away from the cause or the source of the conflict and form a narrator's perspective of safe verbalization without feelings of blame or guilt. They tend to include more details, such as reasons for the altercation, and why they engaged in violence, abusive discourse, bullying, or cultural discrimination. Their ability to role-play different scenarios and present various viewpoints provides a natural progression in analyzing the dilemma, much like assessing bits and pieces of literature or historical realism when attempting to understand the basis of societal problems and the ongoing wars between countries based on cultural and religious differences. Students presented with a realistic scenario of events or emotions, feelings, and behaviors quickly learn to identify with common needs or to explore situations discussed in class, novels, films, or writings in a pragmatic light within an educational setting. Teachers can model and provide examples of leadership, character, forbearance, and cultural morals that highlight cooperation, coexistence, and collaboration among individuals and nations.

So often, patterns are set at an early age in the home environment, and many young people tend to carry out their feelings of low self-esteem and failure through inappropriate acts of conduct in school settings. Being in control of a situation or manipulating other students through threats or harassments brings a sense of power that many young people feel places them in a better position for acceptance and acknowledgment by their peers. One case in point, focused on a junior who referred to himself as "Big Mac." Knowledge, education, and studying for SAT's were not his prime area of interest. Rather, Big Mac was a bona fide delinquent, with time spent in detention centers and jail facilities. He firmly believed in violence and using force at whim to achieve his goals. The young man's perspective on life formed at a very early age and was not tempered by limits or standards of acceptance by society. Big Mac handled conflicts, differences, and disputes by imitating an air of diplomacy, including firm handshakes and smiles to his victims. He also employed firm "backing" or physical support from fellow students who were either coerced or belittled into gang-like involvement with Big Mac as their leader. Out of fear, retribution, or peer acceptance, easily swayed youngsters and those relating to violence as a natural way of life gathered around their new leader, cintributing to an atmosphere of internal terror and external conflicts.

The sense of "family" that ensued within the gang-like atmosphere soon faced opposition and pressure from school officials, administrators, counselors, teachers, parents, and security police. Those students participating in altercations and fighting on school grounds received the appropriate punishments based on a "zero tolerance" policy advocating campus nonviolence. Through subsequent mediation counseling and anger management training, students worked toward identifying the reasons for conflict, finding solutions to their problems, and reaching agreement to dissipate the hostility or inappropriate behaviors with fellow peers. Many students, for the first time, came in contact with peaceful choices or options for expressing their feelings, anger, and resentment.

Developing Empathy

Through storytelling or narrative mediation, students willingly took the opportunity to express their views by stepping into another perspective and acknowledging relevant feelings, social norms, family values, and peer relationships. The identification of issues became an important tool to help understand the lack of tolerance and humanity for others. As cyclical patterns emerged rooted in peer acceptance, environmental, or cultural issues, participants found a new appreciation and a basic acceptance for common goals, dreams, and desires. They shared their stories in an atmosphere that became calm, safe, and communicative. Their uninterrupted words presented an opportunity for thought, growth, change, and progress to take place. (See figure 4.1.)

Individual members of the gang recanted and demonstrated signs of confusion, apology, and forgiveness for previous actions. Although their sense of decency and moral judgment was clouded by moments of pressure and manipulation from gang involvement, they felt no ill will or hatred toward those they taunted or bullied. Big Mac was the

Figure 4.1 The Pattern of Narrative Mediation

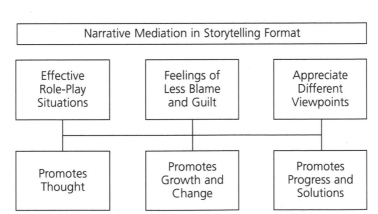

only student who closed the door to compromise and negotiation through conflict resolution communication. He was firmly committed to his atmosphere of violence and his ethics of intolerance and manipulation. The separation of this young man from his actions of narrow-mindedness, disobedience, and rebelliousness only served to intensify his negative coping skills and his affirmation of violence. He played the role of neighborhood champion in his own mind and ended up living out his ingrained patterns of inappropriate and destructive behavior incarcerated.

Without the benefit of narrative mediation, individuals continue to experience guilt and blame for violating society's standards, which reinforces old patterns of rigidity and acts to break down any balance of impartiality and tolerance. Instead of peaceful progress, society feels the negative effects of copy-cat acts of prejudice and violence. conflict resolution communication offers valued mediation techniques and effective communication strategies to encourage a lifetime of positive choices and behaviors. Young people form new coping skills to work toward successful negotiations as they commit to nonviolence and tolerance.

By identifying issues, using narrative mediation to reframe event perspectives, listening with respect and understanding, and working toward a mutual solution, students take responsibility for their own actions. A safer learning environment becomes apparent as students learn from their mistakes. A new sense of empowerment unfolds as new attitudes and new behavior patterns emerge on campus. The end-of-year evaluation of the mediation program revealed that more than 50 percent of all altercations on the secondary level were lessened by conflict resolution practices and that most conflicts were based on rumors, lack of information, "he said/she said" statements, and misunderstandings

The conflict resolution communication program models and incorporates the processes and problem-solving skills of mediation, negotiation, and collaboration. Educator Peter Maurer integrates conflict resolution skills into his daily classroom lessons in a Detroit, Michigan, public school. In his article, "Another View: School Discipline Needs New, Updated Lesson Plan," Maurer believes that "defiant, dangerous, and disrespectful students can literally destroy a classroom and endanger student and staff alike. . . . It's time to set a minimum standard of acceptable human behavior and learning ability by introducing a series of conflict resolution classes, manners, stress management, peer mentoring, etc." (Maurer, 1998, pp. A11–A12). Students need the communication skills and negotiation techniques that will enable them to diffuse conflicts effectively and relieve stress peacefully. Trained mediators can affect the level of violence and promote a sense of safety in schools by facilitating conflict resolution processes, communication techniques, and problem-solving skills.

Another successful breakthrough in conflict resolution practices focuses on the narrative mediation approach to problem solving and effective negotiation. Winslade and Cotter developed a retelling incident technique in their article "A Narrative Approach to the Practice of Mediation," in *The Negotiation Journal*. Their approach detaches the conflicting party from the emotional side of the story, separating feelings of blame and guilt from the narrator's point of view. Narrative therapy has become a leading approach to problem solving in mediation. Through the application of storytelling and detailed responses, individual narratives are heard and acknowledged with greater clarity and understanding by conflicting parties. Mediators rely on the positive effects of narrative thinking to create and develop different perspectives by which conflict can be analyzed, comprehended, and resolved. (See figure 4.2.)

Because conflict scenarios originate in the conceptions of individual's needs and desires, successful negotiation techniques focus on signifi-

Figure 4.2 Positive Effects of Narrative Mediation

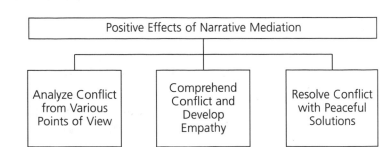

cantly satisfying and finding solutions to basic human needs. Win-win solutions that meet the needs of all conflicting parties become the essential element in problem-solving mediation (Winslade & Cotter, 1999).

Public concerns center on the neutrality and objectivity of the mediator in problem-solving conflict situations. Is it feasible for the mediator to remain value-free, outside time and space, and to abstain from bias and judgment intervention? Does the mediator serve all parties impartially and avoid the adversarial or advocacy role? Does the content in dispute and the mediation process take on the influence of a third-party mediator using interpretive methods based on personal attitudes, experiences, evidence, and beliefs? An experienced mediator remains impartial throughout the process and encourages the development and unfolding of key issues through a nonaggressive narrative approach. The development of a narrative approach to mediation addresses these issues and creates a perspective of events within the context of larger stories to be analyzed through a cultural context (Winslade & Cotter, 1999).

A narrative approach to mediation allows the participants to see conflict, not stemming from dysfunctional patterns, but being created by cultural differences and personal experiences (Winslade & Cotter, 1999). By understanding and exploring the nature of inequalities, conflicting parties can set the issues within a narrative field and then resolve them through a practical approach that works through diversity and differences. Phyllis Kritek confirmed this negotiating perspective by outlining the approach of negotiating at uneven tables. She based her experience, perspective, inequalities, manipulation, and gender stereotypes on personal encounters in health-related fields. By redefining the role of negotiation, participants minimize manipulation and inequality, which led to successful narrative techniques for resolving professional conflicts. She offers narrative thinking presented honestly, sincerely, and collectively to support narrative negotiation sessions and alternative conflict solutions.

The mediator must apply successful strategies from a narrative perspective to explore the stories behind the participants' conflict situation. Alternative stories must be identified and developed through interactive dialogue that advances nonadversarial narratives (Kritek,

1994). By inviting the participants to retell an event within a different frame of reference, the mediator reduces guilt and blame overshadowing the conflict and raises the understanding of responsibility for the conflict by the participants. The process detaches blame from the particular party and assigns it to the narrative itself (Kritek, 1994). Both parties hear themselves and one another move away from the conflict story and toward understanding and mutual respect—the story-in-progress that leads to resolution and agreements. The narrative approach of retelling the story enabled students to step away from the anger and hurt of conflict. They are able to concentrate on the expression of language that moves them to a fresh perspective and an agreed-upon solution.

Discourse involves the sharing of words and meanings that affect the interaction between people. The conversation or active speech events rely heavily on the development and communication of social practices, personal experience, and structural arrangements. Through discourse, individuals form perspectives based on knowledge, belief, and narrative meaning that uncover the very nature of a conflict (Winslade & Monk, 2000, p. 42). Determining the worth of a particular wording or utterance is accomplished by investigating its context. By actively applying a "users' language," even within cultural presuppositions, the speaker contributes to sentence comprehension in and through the use of context. The use of language in context links the communicative response to the actual telling of the story. Conflict resolution communication specialists extract the meaning of discourse to help identify the issues of conflict.

Earliest Recorded Mediated Discourse

Alessandro Duranti stressed the importance of responsibility or agency in the earliest recorded mediated discourse or interpretation of speech in the Samoan culture in *From Grammar to Politics*. A hierarchy of social interaction determined the role of the mediator and the participant's involvement rather than in reconstructing the speaker's intentions. Words were interpreted as deeds, activities, or tasks within a social order.

While studying and collecting data on the hierarchical levels, or inter-active relationships of the Samoan culture, he identified their social structure through the power of authority, expertise, and responsibility. The individual became important in terms of his or her position to fit a specific role, or to follow the tendency to obscure the individual in favor of a public and positional role. The fono, or particular Samoan speech event, defined through verbal performance by professional speechmakers, accessed political decision making in the village, the subvillage, or the tribal district. Opinions were framed on behalf of the group. Talk and interpretation depended on the norms of a given time and place, and were seen as activities or tasks giving assigned roles of responsibility to others (Duranti, 1994).

The speech events were framed around a common problem or social action coordinated by linguistic performance leading to assumptions and various outcomes or political events. The verbal interactions within the fono held people accountable for their words and actions. The matai, or the legislative body of chiefs and orators, made or broke the laws, and took on new conflicts leading to mediated and compromised solutions. These powerful groups of individuals controlled each other's political actions through cautious, humble, vague, forceful, or direct be-havior. The Samoans, who were aware of the power of words in public circumstances, were careful and skillful in presenting their viewpoints. The tulafale, orators and talking chiefs, used various strategies to deal with the power of words in a context-creating sense. Their right and duty included representing others in ceremonial manners, such as rites of passage or public gift-giving instances. The tulafale also acted as me-diators and spokespersons in political conflicts. The chiefs rewarded the orators for carrying out their responsibilities, but they also pro-tected themselves from retaliation, punishment, or blame by saying little and remaining vague in community conflict situations. Their views were most often expressed after many of the problems were either solved or debated. Meaning and interpretation depended on the collective response or social behavior of the audience without notice to the speaker's intentional meaning. Context was defined through the co-operative language usage of the culture or society at hand (Duranti, 1994).

Samoan Local Theory and the Samoan Theory of Task interpreted words through the understanding and controlling of social relations, rather than assuming what a person meant intentionally. Language was analyzed through people's actions and what they thought about themselves, not for classification. These assessments focused on actual situations spinning off meaningful speech acts, rather than focusing on the people themselves. During the kava, or opening ceremony, the orator delivered a formal speech, or a lauga, with a rather vague reference to the meeting's agenda, or mata 'upu a le fono, at the end of the address. The senior orator, Moe'ono-M, became the chairman of the meeting and took responsibility for the agenda, which described facts and the performance about the world. If the fealofani, or ideal social harmony or "mutual love" within the community, was in danger of disruption, the orator would be reprimanded for being too direct or for expressing a wrong opinion contrary to most (Duranti, 1994, p. 64). The full-time members would speak their mind on an issue within the ethics of public speaking following the orators, who often spoke first on behalf of their chief who would save face if he changed his opinion. The Samoans accepted responsibility for taking part in a particular social act, committed to a public act, facing political defeat, or losing face. The consequences of their actions were based on the results of the behavior, rather than on the quality of the act. The Samoan speaker learned to deal directly with the circumstances created by his words and with the reality created by his speech.

The Samoan community provided social control, task accomplishment, and reciprocal recognition or cooperative achievement. People were held responsible for their own intentions reflected through acts, words, consequences, and public images, rather than individual intentions. The practice of communication within the Samoan theory led to a better understanding of past and present culture, and a better relationship between the sender's intentions and the receiver's interpretation of meaning. Speaking to others, for others, and through others often became problematic in analyzing one another's behavior within a social context and in creating the foundations of the hierarchy of the social order (Duranti, 1994, p. 101). Mediating activities became increasingly important and useful in helping to organize speech experiences, social interactions, and the practicality of carrying them out.

In other words, the earliest form of narrative mediation most likely developed its origin in the importance of communication among native tribes. In order to understand the issues at hand, different perspectives of the altercation were presented and interpreted by listening, identifying issues and related details, accepting responsibility for the actions surrounding the conflict, and deciding on a course of action that would lead to a peaceful resolution for all participants involved. Narrative conflict resolution communication represents somewhat similar creative communication techniques to help separate the conflicting party from the emotions surrounding the altercation, as well as distinguish feelings of blame and guilt from the narrator's point of view.

5

Negotiation: The Opposing Sides of Verbal and Nonverbal Communication

"I have often regretted my speech, never my silence."
— Anonymous

Effective negotiation takes the commitment and the willingness of two conflicting parties to apply verbal and nonverbal cues, with the help of third-party involvement, in bringing about possible solutions. Nonverbal communication can contribute valuable support to the goal of successful resolution in the process of addressing conflict and employing peaceful alternatives. Often what is not verbally stated but inferred through body movements, distance, and timing correlates to the victory or demise of significant negotiation. By identifying the problematic issues, narrating the sequence of events, using active listening skills, applying problem-solving techniques, diffusing the escalating conflict, and working toward a mutually acceptable agreement, the disputants rely on their ability to communicate, both verbally and nonverbally, in negotiating a settlement.

Nonverbal cues as they relate to the negotiation process focus on facial expressions, gestures, head nods, foot movements, open and closed body positioning, eye contact, touching, posturing, and physical appearance. The particular inferences associated with nonverbal cues often "speak louder than words" when attempting to align opposing viewpoints and defuse conflicts. The effects of nonverbal communication on negotiation procedures are particularly striking when it comes to human emotion. In working through conflict, nonverbal cues affect a range of emotions, including happiness, sadness, fear, surprise, anger, disgust, contempt, pride, embarrassment, guilt, and jealousy. These emotional factors play an important role in escalating conflicts, prioritizing issues, employing active listening techniques, and communicating effectively. The interplay of nonverbal communication in conflict is too often used to accentuate individual differences rather than enhance human strengths. These nonverbal cues—often based in cultural diversity—are observable in the workplace, the classroom setting, and in the routine of everyday life.

Practices of Negotiation

Negotiation is defined as a "conciliatory process, or act of bringing together conflicting parties to settle their disputes, in a consensual and private setting with minimal third-party involvement" (Yarn, 1999, p. 314). Mediation, therefore, at its most basic level is facilitated negotiation (Yarn, 1999). The mediator or impartial third party facilitates negotiations toward a resolution between disputants. The disputants remain responsible for negotiating a settlement. The mediator's role is to assist the process in ways acceptable to the disputants, including providing a forum for negotiations, convening the negotiations, helping the disputants find areas of common ground for resolution, offering alternatives, supervising the bargaining, and then drafting the final settlement (Leeson & Johnston, 1988).

Mediation occupies the space between negotiation and arbitration along a continuum of dispute resolution processes (Yarn, 1999, p. 155). The arbitrator, unlike the mediator, renders a determination in settlement of the dispute after giving the parties an opportunity to present their evidence and arguments (p. 28). The mediator, however, assists in the negotiations and is empowered to intervene in the dialogue and to use powers of persuasion to help the parties reach a mutually acceptable outcome without ordering a formal court decision prescribed by law (p. 276).

The experienced mediator relies on effective communication skills and the presence of nonverbal cues in facilitating active listening and appreciation of different viewpoints on the part of all parties. Role-plays and improvisations help the conflicting parties address one another's perspectives from a different angle. The parties are urged to move their emotions and feelings aside as they identify and clarify the issues on the table. Through paraphrasing or restating the goals of the session and what was discussed, the mediator helps the parties work out the details of the negotiations and formulate a working agreement.

Interaction of Nonverbal Cues

Attention to the presence of nonverbal cues in a conflict is essential. A "discrepancy often exists between what the speaker is thinking or feeling and what he or she is actually saying" (Scott, 1990, p. 119). Communication is likely to be misinterpreted or discredited by the very message someone thinks they are communicating due to the person's nonverbal cues. One party may develop a sense of distrust, negativity, or inappropriate feelings if they question whether the other party means what is said. For example, if nervousness, hesitancy, or lack of eye contact is expressed through body language, it may be interpreted as insincerity or incompatibility. A disparity between the intended message and its presentation becomes evident and may lead to further conflict. "Body language is often unwilled—but it can be controlled" (Scott, 1990, p. 100). By acknowledging the presence of nonverbal cues and their tendency for misinterpretation, conflicting parties can realign their communication skills to help defuse conflict (Scott, 1990).

Nonverbal communication plays a significant role in the dynamics of the negotiation process. According to experts in the communication field, about 55 percent of received information originates from the nonverbal communication that accompanies a spoken message, including body movements and facial gestures; 38 percent comes from the voice, pitch, tone, and sounds; and only 7 percent draws from the content of the message (Scott, 1990, p. 100). (See figure 5.1.)

To reduce or even eliminate a discrepancy between nonverbal and verbal content, the parties can apply gestures, tones, and body

Figure 5.1 Discrepancy Between Nonverbal and Verbal Communication

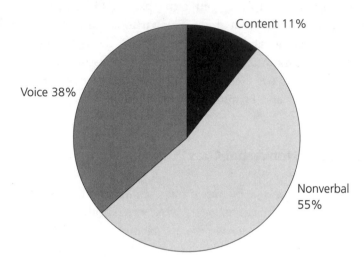

movements in a nonthreatening way. Misconstrued communication is avoided by directing nonverbal cues and body language in the following positive ways (Scott, 1990):

1. Indicate a smile of friendliness rather than using a cold, hostile tone of voice, clenched fists, or a movement away from anger or dislike.
2. Proclaim a message of trust and a close, warm relationship by avoiding a hesitant manner and shifting eye contact, both of which suggest a lack of confidence or sincerity.
3. Show self-confidence and efforts toward reconciliation by shaking hands without being aggressive or using angry stares, halting mannerisms, and physical acts of aloofness and indifference.

Kinesic Movements

The study of communication and messages received through body movements is called *kinesics*. The interactive nature of body language generally includes gestures, movements of the body (limbs, hands, head, feet, and legs), facial expressions (smiles), eye behavior (blinking, direction and length of gaze, and pupil dilation), and posture (Knapp & Hall, 1997, p. 9). Gestures, for example, used for emphasis to show size, distance, and shape and those that recreate bodily actions (pantomimes) are nonverbal. American Sign Language, however, is linguistic and verbal using adaptors and illustrators to convey nonverbal messages. The voice becomes nonverbal when it communicates analogically through grunts, screams, giggles, or vocal inflection during speech, but not when it reflects the spoken word. Many messages are nebulous or fall into a gray area of being both verbal and nonverbal (Anderson, 1999, pp. 4–5).

Messages of power and dominance are often exploited during conflict resolution negotiation sessions. High-power figures can manipulate and control others seeking solutions to conflict on any level from international to interpersonal. Individual or group status reveals itself through kinesic movements. Positioning at "uneven tables" of negotiation may grant more individual space to those holding more power, whereas tension, serving another person, lowering one's body or bowing in the presence of another reflects subordination. Larger and more frequent gesturing communicates power, including pointing, or lowering the protruding jaw and eyebrows, which are also perceived as rude and angry behavior, respectively. Relaxation is a sign of dominance, while smiling is seen as a submissive behavior. Happy, confidant expressions are powerful, as well as more overall eye contact, whereas fearful or confused expressions and averting eye contact and blinking are subordinate (Anderson, 1999, p. 330).

Proxemics

Proxemics is the study of interactive communication at close distances between individuals. Interpersonal distance and body orientation also serve as important nonverbal indicators of power and status in conflicting situations. Body orientation between two communicators moves between the most direct position of face-to-face contact to a more indirect position of angling or leaning forward toward or backward from an individual. Persons of high status received the most direct contact while women and persons of lower status received the least notice by other persons. Lower-status people generally allot high-profile individuals more personal space and power. Eisenberg and Smith (1971) maintain that the power to defend one's own territory and the right to invade another person's space are certain signs of dominance and prestige while the prerogative to invade someone else's space lies with people of high power and status (Anderson, 1999, p. 317). Closer distances convey more dominance while excessive dominance is viewed as a personal violation. Subordinates, divorcing spouses, disputing employees and employers, parents and children, doctors and patients, doctors and nurses, lovers, and friends must all be careful not to "cross the line" or step into another's territorial boundaries and take the chance of escalating conflicts. Personal grievances and "getting back" at the other person often clouds the issues and results in "lose-lose" situations for all parties involved. Attempts at effective compromise and resolution practices diminish until a mutual respect and a willingness to cooperate among all parties is restored within a safe atmosphere of voluntary negotiation.

Haptics or tactile communication is identified through the power of touch and reflects the most intimate of the nonverbal codes arousing professional, social, or intimate sexual feelings (Anderson, 1999, p. 50). Communication through the sense of touch is considered to be the most intimate and the most powerful form of nonverbal communication (p. 318).

During narrative mediation, hurt feelings, emotions, and intimate feelings are often revealed in the form of anger, distrust, disgust, threats, and insults when exposure of a physical, abusive, or emotional altercation arises. Sometimes, even the respondents still feel or relive intimate moments with the conflicting party reflecting companionship, love, reassurance, and bonding. A dichotomy of intimate and isolated feelings must be recognized and neutralized in order for the mediator to move the parties toward identifying and acknowledging the true issues that need to be resolved to lessen the tension and diffuse the conflict at hand. Nonverbal cues present in the negotiation session are recognized and analyzed by an experienced third-party to bring the respondents together on the issues and toward a win-win solution.

Chronemics

The concept of time is an important commodity with most individuals. Everyday lives, including activities, appointments, vacations, meetings, and school and work-related responsibilities revolve around "having precious little time" or having "too much time on our hands." Chronemics is the study of the way we structure time and the meanings we attach to time during interpersonal interaction (Anderson, 1999, p. 63). The possession of time, however, forms a close association with power and status, and directs our communicative behavior within the environment.

Those individuals of more affluent means may have more control and power over the duration of time they wait for goods and services than those individuals on welfare, in state health-care facilities, or those remaining in employment lines. As status increases, waiting time tends to decrease. "The person who can get a doctor's appointment on short notice is either very important or near death" (Anderson, 1999, p. 321). Chronemic patterns of "turn-taking" talk time are also evidenced with persons of power and status. Dominant individuals talk more and for longer periods of time. They may also attempt to control communication in situations where the other person is never given the chance to speak or to express his or her feelings. They may ask questions in a rhetorical manner, never expecting a response, and impose their will or point of view on others. Power in conflicting situations tends to escalate tension and cause greater resentment. The high-status person may easily initiate a conversation or discussion and terminate it at will by walking away, redirecting the focus of the dialogue, or using gestures to end the meeting. High-status organizations, institutions, and businesses award individuals more control and power over time, thus enabling them to gain further power and prestige over others and within the organizations (Anderson, 1999).

Emotional Factors

Persons with power and greater maneuverability tend to influence the direction of negotiation or conflict resolution alternatives. Their perspectives and influence can determine the terms of financial support, availability of visitation privileges, division of material goods and services, among others, and set the tone of the negotiations through fear, intimidation, or reprisal involving conflicting parties. Emotional factors play a significant role in the development of working through altercations and arriving at a workable solution for all parties. A "fine line" divides the strong bonds of love from hate when the party's relationship sours or becomes upset by outside forces. As negotiation procedures unfold, an experienced facilitator successfully enables the participants to "park" their emotions and hurt feelings while they concentrate on identifying the issues and finding solutions.

Although emotions are relevant in relationships and run the gamut from hot to cold, their impact on the individuals can be tremendous and long lasting. Disputants sometimes attempt to manipulate and hold onto the other party through nonverbal emotional power plays that can affect the direction of the negotiations. Anger, surprise, fear, sadness, disgust, and contempt are perceived and interpreted through eye contact, facial expressions, open and closed body movements, head nods, and gestures. Taking advantage of others' vulnerabilities or wounding their pride can end negotiations and even enable further manipulation and escalation of the conflict and opposing perspectives. The parties are then focused on ways of "hurting one another" rather than on finding ways to deal successfully with the situation in a win-win atmosphere.

Environment

Physical surroundings impact the way individuals interact with others nonverbally. In cities where space is more limiting and crowding exists, people tend to move into others' personal territory. A greater incidence of violent crimes and violations of personal rights are noted in police reports and crime statistics. In the workplace, many employees may feel too rushed or too busy to get to know the people they work with on a daily basis. Passing someone in the corridor or sharing an elevator may result in a blank stare, nodding of the head, tipping of the head, looking down at the floor or toward the ceiling, or ignoring eye contact with fellow employees, altogether. Harsh feelings may develop into altercations, resulting in a need for resolution services. Human resource departments may institute mediation service programs in many businesses and corporations for conflicts that develop in the workplace between the employers and the employees. Greater productivity, financial gains, and more harmonious interactions among the working force are documented benefits of such programs as they provide coping skills and strategies to personnel through negotiation and resolution practices.

Before communication effectively helps to heal the anger of the disputants, nonverbal signs or signals of aggression need to be broken down and turned into constructive remarks and opportunities of creative dialogue. Disputants need to show positive body movements and positions by facing one another without turning away or tapping their fingers or fists on the table indicating frustration, boredom, or total indifference. Foot stomping or consistent tapping on the floor, playing with a purse, a book, a watch, or twirling one's hair also indicates a sense of nervousness or a lack of patience with the other person or with the resolution process itself. They also tend to limit personal accounts of narrative mediation and act as time restraints.

One of the most difficult nonverbal acts of conciliation for many of the participants to observe is shaking hands with the other person to signal that the conflict is over. The participants will more readily imply that the altercation will never happen again because they want to stay out of trouble and relieve stressful situations. When asked, however, if the olive branch can be extended in a sincere manner by looking at one another directly and offering a handshake, faces suddenly tighten up, posture becomes stiffened, eyes widen, and hands often disappear in pockets or behind backs. At that point, the following example of road rage by using nonverbal cues and gestures can be shared:

Two motorists are driving home from work on the beltway at rush hour. One motorist is driving at the speed limit while the fellow directly behind appears to be in a great hurry, and tries to pass the first driver without success. Finally, the second driver is able to move to the left lane when the slower driver also moves to the left, which enrages the faster driver so he attempts to pass the slower driver on the right side. Once again, the slower driver inadvertently blocks the passage of the faster driver by moving into the right-hand lane. Finally, the faster driver pulls next to the slower driver and indicates through direct eye contact that he wants to communicate with the other driver by lowering their car windows, simultaneously. The slower driver, hesitantly, lowers his window only to be given an obscene gesture and an inappropriate and disgusting "off color" term. The faster driver now speeds away.

After closing his window, the slower driver feels violated by the actions of the other motorist, and decides that no one has the right to act that way toward him. He decides to catch up to the faster driver, make direct eye contact, and communicate his thoughts through their open windows. By a miracle, the driver does just that. Once both windows are open and the faster driver is now looking at the other driver, the slower motorist says: " . . ."

At the turning point of the narrative, ask the participants what they would do in this particular conflict situation. They appear ready to speak at the same time and, most often, mimic what the other has offered as a possible solution. They offer repeated statements mirroring inappropriate actions of the drivers inducing further escalation of the conflict. However, the drivers actually responded in a very different way to the road rage incident:

. . . The slower motorist says: "I just wanted to say that I'm sorry and that I had no idea I was blocking your way." The faster motorist appears surprised by his open-mouth and wide-eyed look, and says: "Hey, I'm sorry, too. I shouldn't have insulted you with my hot-tempered actions."

Within moments, the participants through the powerful touch of "shaking hands" generally extend the act of forgiveness and acceptance. By finding ways to break the tension and diffuse the conflict, negotiation practices leave lasting effects on future problem-solving situations.

Active Listening Techniques

Nonverbal communication plays a decisive role in the active listening process of negotiation. Acknowledging the process of listening with the intent to hear and to understand the other person's views and their perspectives emphasizes a closer bond between the disputants. Direct eye contact, head nods, smiles, grins, open and closed body positioning, or leaning toward or away from the speaker, caressing an arm or shoulder, wiping away a tear, or offering audible signals of agreement or disagreement suggest to the speaker that the listener did indeed heard.

Often, just knowing that the other hears makes an immeasurable difference in moving forward to a possible solution and agreement. Although the effects of verbal and nonverbal communication interact with one another, active listening promotes effective negotiation efforts. The interplay of verbal and nonverbal communication in the process of conflict resolution offers a stimulus-response pattern of effectively diffusing conflicts and bringing about negotiated agreements. Nonverbal cues and signals allow the disputants to filter their feelings and reactions openly in a safe environment of third-party intervention. By helping the parties brainstorm and problem-solve in areas of disagreement, the facilitator can emphasize the unspoken words of nonverbal communication and elicit different perspectives through role-plays and simulations. By addressing intimate feelings and responses through kinesic movements, proxemics, and chronemic factors, stressing power, status, and influence, third-party intervention can move the conflicting parties through the dynamic process of uncovering and dealing with the real issues.

The goal of negotiation and mediation practices is to diffuse the conflict, facilitate possible solutions, and encourage mutual agreement reflecting the needs of both sides. The interaction of nonverbal cues within the negotiation process influences how the problem is addressed, the issues identified, and the solution to the conflict determined. Often what is not verbally stated but, instead, inferred through body movements, distance, and timing correlates to the success or demise of effective negotiation.

Nonverbal communication intermingled with verbal communication enhances and strengthens the resolution process.

6

The Brutality of Bullying

"If we cannot now end our differences, at least we can help make the world safe for diversity."
— John Fitzgerald Kennedy

The effects of being maltreated, maligned, and harassed in schools across the country are being observed more frequently by professionals in the form of bullying. Students are singled out, discriminated against, and treated with intolerance and disrespect. Their personal space, rights, responsibilities, and values are being undermined by those bullies who wish to use power and control as a manipulative tool to widen the differences, to create dissent among others, and to spread chaos throughout the halls of learning. By being impervious to cultural traditions, diversity, multicultural morals, and ethical standards, bullies find themselves limited by prejudice and hatred. Safe surroundings of learning become camps of fear and worry for those victims who are unabashedly devalued and dehumanized in front of peers. Too often, those tormented by cruelty remain too afraid to speak up for fear of being the next targets of violence.

The alarming number of school-related incidents across the country involving violence demands a careful look at the origins of conflict and ways to prevent it peacefully. James Gilligan, a Harvard psychiatrist, spent years interviewing murderers in Massachusetts, and concluded the following: "Nothing stimulates violence as powerfully as the experience of being shamed and humiliated" (Dority, 1999, p. 4). One of the most common denominators of teenagers who are harassed, bullied, and excluded by other students, cliques, or family members is low self-esteem and lack of self-confidence. They need to talk, identify troubling issues in their lives, and work through their problems in a safe environment.

Often, students lack the communication and listening skills needed to deal with their differences effectively. Conflict resolution communication programs need to be implemented in every public school system across the nation and be made available to students in elementary through the secondary levels. These programs can reduce the tension of students while enabling them to solve conflicts and negotiate gang disputes, family troubles, and neighborhood problems (Smith, 1993). Students need to be armed, not with automatic weapons and firearms, but with effective coping skills and anger management techniques provided by professionals who can successfully convey the fundamental processes of conflict resolution communication. Schools need to be safe havens of learning that promote the richness of cultural diversity, character education, and tolerance for all students.

The brutality of bullying is characterized by a loss of self-discipline, a failure to control actions, words, and impulses, and a deficit of commitment or desire to complete an admirable goal through worthy means. A lack of respect for authority, self, property, and community and a total disregard for accountability, obligations, and duties reflect the nature of the aggressor. Such behavior can scar victims leaving them with a lifetime of pain and grief that often opens them up to a cyclical pattern of abuse and intolerance for others. The inflicted cruelty on those being bullied becomes an open wound resisting treatment or soothing remedies if the conflict remains unresolved. The reasons for the small-minded behavior and the acts of remorse, sorrow, or apology go unnoticed because they continue to be overlooked, inconsequential, and ignored by the perpetrator. For consistent progress to be made in obliterating the effects of bullying, the internal causes or reasons for the inappropriate actions of the bully must be revealed, understood, and removed. This vital condition requires that the intimidator acknowledge his or her old patterns of behavior and work to establish healthy coping strategies that lead to a peaceful coexistence in today's society.

The bully, however, often resists change, foresight, and a leveling of power. The attention and focus provoked by the abuser adds a false dimension or impression of control and value to the bully's behavior pattern. Intimidated by the perpetrator's aggression and not willing to fall victim to physical violence, the intended prey abides by the demands and the will of their captor. A dual behavior pattern, both of the bully and the victim, tends to become cyclical, reinforced by environmental, family, peer, or abusive factors. Patterns solidified by repeated social and cultural morals need to be examined, analyzed, and evaluated for their motivators. The dishonor granted to the bully by the community reflects a sense of self-deprecation that is incomplete and without truth or respect. The violence extended by the bully through thoughts, actions, and words projects a sense of irresponsible and unnecessary cruelty toward the diversity prominent in society. (See figure 6.1.)

The process of conflict resolution communication adds a powerful dimension to breaking the pattern of unacceptable behaviors and discovering the foundation of the conflict and anger prevalent in violent actions. By examining the profile or characteristics of the bully and the victim, by identifying the most frequent or widespread school scenarios for violence, and by treating the social and the cultural erosion leading

Figure 6.1 The Brutality of Bullying: The Victim

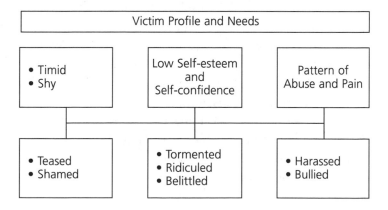

to those scenarios, trained conflict resolution communication specialists successfully integrate mediation strategies with communication skills to effectively reduce bullying and its negative effects. Identifying the source of the problem and applying the essential treatment to eliminate the cycle of viciousness brings a sense of closure and resolve to school-based altercations.

Actions of the Perpetrator

Profiling the bully and the victim and identifying repetitive patterns of behavior based on environment, culture, peer pressure, family influence, and abusive situations leads to early identification and helpful intervention techniques to break the cycle of school violence. The aggressive nature and threats, manipulative actions, and the power of the perpetrator's words encased in harassments, rumors, and third-party hearsay raise the image of the bully to that of a marksman ready to annihilate his or her target with utter or complete control. By bending the spirit and breaking the backbone of the intended victim, the bully maintains his or her place among followers who repeat and clone the inappropriate behavior patterns of the tormenter. Doctors Leonard Eron and Rowell Huesmann at the University of Illinois–Chicago believe that aggressive behavior can be learned by watching others act aggressively, including viewing aggression on television, being rewarded for acting aggressively, and being treated aggressively (Fried & Fried, 1996, p. 89). Those who believe that this type of behavior could be emulated, valued, inspired, or imitated by others with any degree of acceptance by society are misled. Initially, the bully may gain an illusory sense of self-confidence from these feelings of power, or ignore practical warnings about such socially unacceptable behavior. By ignoring the warnings or the consequences of sustained actions, the bully loses all perspective of cause and effect and remains resistant to change. The bully maintains destructive behavior patterns and continues to use violence, wreaking havoc and promoting isolationism that contributes to the decay of society.

From the profile of the abuser, we see a person in urgent need of recognizing and understanding the reasons leading to aggressive behavior.

A diminishing connection with society imbues the tormentor with an intolerance for cultural differences and individual human needs.

Seeking intense reactions from his victims in the form of fear, shock, and distress, the bully continues to impugn "in-your-face" behavior. (See figure 6.2.) Considerations for controlling the cycle of violent behavior must include the following (Fried & Fried, 1996, p. 29):

- Inappropriate behavior is unacceptable.
- Physical and verbal bullying is a concern.
- Reports of bullying must be taken seriously.
- Alternatives to fighting need to be discussed with young males and their fathers or male role models.
- Young men need to know that they can gain approval without resorting to violence.
- Firearms in the hands of children should be banned.
- Media violence should be challenged.
- Parents should exert authority over the quantity and quality of exposure to violent programming by their children.

The cycle continues until effective intervention techniques are applied as identified in the conflict resolution communication model.

Figure 6.2 The Brutality of Bullying: The Abuse or the Bully

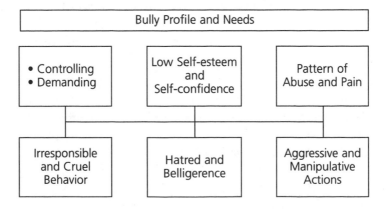

Turning Point at Columbine

School tragedies, such as the innocent killings at Columbine High School in Littleton, Colorado, in April 1999, and the rash of copy-cat violent acts occurring at schools across the nation bring immediate attention and concern for the safety and the welfare of student populations and an awareness of tolerance and the expected deference to cultural diversity found in today's institutions of higher learning. A "wake-up" call for educators, parents, and students led to spontaneous and sudden meetings, conferences, protests, and changes in the implementation and maintenance of our public education system.

What changed in the last twenty years of educating our youth? What made young people so angry? When did violence take on the look of semi-automatic weapons and pipe bombs? Why were gangs so prevalent on school campuses? Why did students feel compelled to identify their allegiance with power, status, and manipulation by wearing bandanas, engraved belts, colored jackets, or trench coats? What prompted American youth to hold teachers and students hostage, sacrificing innocent lives, and then ending their own lives? Why has aggression penetrated the halls of learning with excessive and impenetrable violence and destruction?

A Wake-Up Call to Action

In a national poll of young people, children ages seven to ten reported a pervasive fear of violence and early death. The same poll indicated widespread experience of crime and violence among teens (*USA Today*, December 7, 1995). The telephone survey of 1,000 eleven- to seventeen-year-olds (margin of error 3 percentage points), and in-person interviews with 120 seven- to ten-year-olds found that 71 percent of children ages seven to ten worry they might get shot or stabbed at school or home and 40 percent of girls ages fourteen to seventeen know someone their age who has been hit or beaten by a boyfriend (Fried & Fried, 1996, p. 18). Associate Dean and Director of the Center for Health Communication at the Harvard School of Public

Health, Jay Winsten, states: "Yesterday's fist fight has become today's shootout. Yesterday's black eye and injured pride is today's gaping two-inch exit wound with internal injuries" (Fried & Fried, 1996, p. 19). Firearms and their availability and accessibility add a new dimension to the war on bullying. The Louis Harris Research firm released a survey in 1993 that stated 59 percent of school children in sixth through twelfth grades say they "could get a handgun if they wanted one." More than a third said they could get one "within an hour." Thirty-five percent of the students polled believe their lives will be cut short because of guns. Violence attributed to handguns will cause more adolescent deaths than illness. The National Center for Health Statistics reports that homicide by firearms is now the second-leading cause of death (after motor vehicle crashes) for fifteen- to nineteen-year-old Caucasians. For African Americans in that age bracket, homicide is the leading cause of death. Altercations over girls, sports-related jackets, sneakers, boyfriends, and so on can end in fatal shootings (Fried & Fried, 1996, p. 20).

The answers are not simple or exact in terms of identifying the sources or origins of the troubles plaguing today's youth. The combination of conflict at home, conflict at school, conflict at work, conflict in relationships, and conflict between strangers stemming from cultural, social, or economic differences all contribute to negative patterns of behavior. By advancing new thought patterns and options, students can choose healthier mindsets and, using conflict resolution communication strategies. face complex choices and difficult times.

Copy-Cat Acts of School Violence

In March 2001, malicious and fatal shootings of two students at Santana High School in Santee, California, by Charles Andrew Williams, a bullied fifteen-year-old and another shooting, just two days later, of a cheerleading co-captain at Bishop Neumann High School in Williamsport, Pennsylvania, by fourteen-year-old Elizabeth Catherine Bush for tormenting and bullying her took place (Boodman, 2001). The effects of bullying and violent behavior erupting from gangs, drugs, and the use of weapons in schools leave scars and inflict long-term consequences (see figure 6.3).

Kevin Dwyer, former president of the National Association of School Psychologists, believes that confronting bullying means confronting deeply ingrained cultural expectations and serious psychological harm. The School Psychologist Association reports the following (Boodman, 2001, HE 15):

- Daily, 160,000 American youths skip school fearing they will be the targets of bullies.
- Children identified as bullies or as victims at age eight were still identified as such at age sixteen.
- Both groups had more emotional problems than other students.
- Bullied students have higher rates of depression, which persist into adulthood.
- Of boys identified as bullies in middle school, 60 percent had at least one criminal conviction by age 24, while 40 percent had three or more convictions.

The University of Colorado at Boulder is administering Blueprints, an antibullying program sponsored by the U.S. Justice Department. The goals of the program include a reduction in bullying by changing the culture of a school, enlisting the active participation of intervening adults, and eliminating harassment and threats (Boodman, HE 13). Professor Dan Olweus from the University of Bergen in Norway de-

Figure 6.3 Conflict Resolution Communication Program Bullying Model

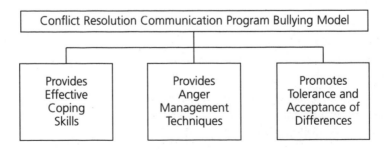

veloped a model antibullying program in 1982 when three young victims of severe school bullying committed suicide within a few months of each other in different parts of the country. Over several years, the program achieved a 50 percent reduction in bullying in Norway and dramatic declines in truancy and vandalism (HE 16). Rumors and miscommunication often lead to conflicts indicating the need for a "re-education" of coping strategies promoting peaceful negotiation and tolerance for diversity.

A U.S. Secret Service study reports that two-thirds of the 41 youths involved in school shootings since 1974 said they had been bullied at school and that revenge was one of their motives. The study noted, "Attackers described experiences of being bullied in terms that approached torment . . . of (being the victim of) behaviors that, if they occurred in the workplace, would meet the legal definitions of harassment" (Broodman, 2001, HE 15).

Taking care of oneself, demonstrating self-defense skills, and knowing how to handle an abuser in all types of situations on school campuses is a tall order for a young person. What was once seen in this country as acceptable behavior in defense of bullying, including kicking and fist fighting is now seen as destructive behavior patterns leading to ongoing conflicts. Healthy coping strategies, effective communication techniques, and applications of anger management and mediation processes must be introduced and implemented through conflict resolution communication.

Conflict Resolution Communication Techniques for Teachers and Administrators

"I have learnt silence from the talkative, toleration from the intolerant, and kindness from the unkind; yet strange, I am grateful to these teachers."
— Kahlil Gibran

The caring nature of the professional educator leads him or her into the world of the student to help that student see it with reality and truth and at the same time promote learning strategies for the student's future. Their specialized training and development enable them to motivate young minds to evaluate situations and apply critical thinking skills as they work toward understanding and tolerance. Instructional techniques tempered with conflict resolution communication patterns for teachers and administrators provide the basic approach in helping students continue to grow and advance their conflict negotiation efforts through peaceful initiatives, voluntary cooperation among disputants, and effective communication skills.

While being sensitive to a variety of learning styles based on a common hegemony of cultures, the educational expert takes on the vital roles of facilitator, listener, nurturer, and peacekeeper. Factors within the school environment, including the teachers' and the administrators' ability to handle their own aggressive feelings, the disciplinary philosophy of the school staff, the willingness of the staff to intervene in student conflicts, class size, and the teacher-to-student ratio work in combination to create a school climate that either discourages or promotes violence (Fried & Fried, 1996, p. 8). Ensuring a safe environment for students to express their perspectives, feelings, narratives, or details of the conflict without harassments or retribution is mandatory for successful conflict resolution communication to take place. The listening skills and mediation techniques taught to the student participants by the educator must be blended with the students' ability to understand and convey not only what is being stated but what is also being literally understood by the other party. An expression of feedback and repetition exercises is applied through the conflict resolution communication program to clarify the communication taking place between the participants.

Some researchers believe that classroom aggression is attributed to the school setting. The incidence of violence increases as the size of school classes increases and the effects of overcrowding, anonymity, and a greater sense of alienation are felt (Fried & Fried, 1996, p. 24). Too often, a "disconnect" or a confused state becomes rooted in the methodology employed by the conflicting parties. They may hear the specific words or phrases used and repeated by the participants but a series of other factors may intervene in their listening process. The power of one's position, the sheer impact of one's size, or the influence of control financially, physically, emotionally, intellectually or spiritually may lessen the opportunity to evaluate what is actually being acknowledged in the mediation session. A variety of factors may upset the prospect for negotiation including hammering on the table, offensive hand gestures, unyielding face-to-face eye contact or unremitting stares, constant verbal interruptions, drooped head or masked face buried on the table, continuous pacing back and forth, covering one's ears, turned away body positioning, incessant humming, talking to oneself, answering rhetorical questions, yelling, and purposely thwarting efforts to resolve differences and disputes peacefully.

One such incident involved a teacher who attempted to bring order to an out-of-control classroom situation by yelling at a group of students and firmly grasping the arm of a female student. When told to report to the office, the student was more concerned with alleviating the teacher's grasp and setting herself free. An inappropriate verbalization materialized between the two as a shoving match escalated into physical violence that was now being egged on by the rallying call of anxious students who experienced metamorphosis from participants to observers. The teacher not only lost control of the learning situation but was in the process of losing her temper and stepping outside the bounds or professional behavior. More out-of-place comments exchanged between the two participants led to the teacher slapping the student's face and the student punching the teacher's chin. Security finally arrived, removed the injured parties, and settled the room down as the bell sounded. Word of the altercation spread quickly around the school campus with strong reactions from the faculty and administrators while student protests emphasized a "violation of their rights to be heard without force or undue harm."

What went wrong? How did this classroom situation escalate to verbal abuse and violence between teacher and student? Did outside or personal factors affect choices that needed to be made swiftly and with the best interests of the students involved? Did the parties attempt any peaceful remedies? Did heated tempers, lack of respect, or the need to "save face" influence destructive choices? Was the opportunity to learn and to grow from being involved in conflict minimized? Had conflict resolution communication training, strategies, and techniques been provided for staff, administrators, and students?

In the past twenty years, the incidence of violence and aggression committed by youth increased dramatically. Some motives are premeditated, accidental, and impulsive while others relate to gang intervention, seek revenge, stem from jealousy, or defy explanation (Fried & Fried, 1996, p. 17). News events in Japan, a country that took pride in its reputation as a safe, low-crime country until recently, notes a rise in serious crime to a 23-year high—the consequence of change in society similar to those experienced in the West. Shocking attacks by strangers and a series of senseless murders involving youths as victims or perpetrators prompted debate in Japan about the upbringing of their youths. A knife-wielding 37-year-old stranger under psychiatric care and heavy tranquilizers killed seven elementary school-aged children and wounded a teacher in Osaka, Japan, before being subdued by teachers and administrators. He entered the school from a playground and without warning murdered seven children as they sat in their second-grade classroom and injured more than 20 others (*The Washington Post*, June 8, 2001).

Strategic Plan Needed

Schools need an administrative strategy in place to deal with an immediate threat to school safety, along with additional lines of communication with professionals who can assist targeted individuals. Guidance counselors, assistant principals, security specialists, teachers, advisors, health professionals, principals, and staff must be trained in the essential elements of conflict resolution communication. They must recognize the early warning signs of a possible perpetrator and those of a victim about to become involved in violence. A "game plan" to maintain safety, to secure the help of professionals on and off campus, and to communicate effectively to alleviate danger and violent activity aimed at the school community must be in place for implementation at any given moment. (See figure7.1.)

Identifying with another's point of view through empathetic analysis, learning to express anger and frustration productively, decreasing socially inappropriate behaviors, providing impulse control strategies and anger management training, increasing social confidence and self-esteem through assertiveness training, social skills rehearsal, and role-play serve as invaluable and interactive approaches to intervention management (Fried & Fried, 1996, p. 103). School violence can erupt on all campuses, urban and rural, and culturally diverse or econom-

Figure 7.1 Conflict Resolution Communication Techniques for Teachers and Administrators

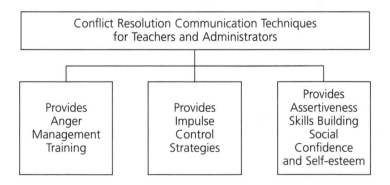

ically affluent or poverty stricken areas without boundaries separating prosperous counties or isolated boroughs. On the average, five school shootings occur yearly on American campuses, a statistic influenced by the availability of semiautomatic weapons (Stern, 2001, p. 151). Effective communication between students, parents, and teachers must be continuous and supplemented by violence prevention programs at every school. Conflict resolution communication as a preventative measure offers a variety of techniques to alleviate danger before it becomes tragic. Recommendations for school administrators, staff, and teachers include the following (Fried & Fried, 1996, p. 156):

- Appoint a committee to determine clear, enforced policies against violence conflict, and bullying practices that hold students accountable for their behavior.
- Create a weapon-free, safe environment for students and teachers.
- Enlist the entire school community, including bus drivers, custodians, cafeteria workers, counselors, principals, coaches, and health professionals to be part of a consistent team that gives the same message: Bullying and inappropriate behavior is unacceptable.
- Be aware of signs of abuse in the home and make appropriate reports to authorities.
- Bring peer abuse prevention curriculum, videos, speakers, and campaigns into the school and community structure.
- Empower witnesses to defend victims, defuse bullies and perpetrators of violent behavior, and support each other; there is power in numbers.
- Give students the attention, information, skills, and support they need.

Because environment, culture, and peer acceptance serve as formidable factors in successful communication, the administrator and teacher must explore a diverse approach to racial, social, and domestic communication. They must be willing to take the lead in bringing the conflicting parties together in the best educational atmosphere and in the safest school surroundings in order to foster a sense of negotiation and resolution. Furthermore, the professional must persuade the students to voluntarily participate in the process, and must find creative ways to dispel their hostility and to ease their differences. The specialist may provide the first opportunity for students to address their disagreements in a positive light. A nonjudgmental feeling of acceptance and a sense of welcome needs to be conveyed to those needing solution skills. All parties need to address the conflicting situation with a seriousness and sincerity in terms of choosing appropriate options for unacceptable behaviors, controlling one's temper through anger management techniques, and successful application of communication and conflict resolution skills.

Warning Signs of Violent Behavior

Dwyer, Osher, and Warger (2000) advocate the use of early warning devices in identifying violent conflict characteristics for individuals before they occur. In their article, "Warning Signs of School Violence," the authors recognize the predictive behavior most likely to lead to violence, and recommend appropriate intervention or professional referral. Imminent warning signs indicate that certain behavior is potentially dangerous or lethal to those expressing harm to anyone. These identified behaviors usually occur in a sequence of events directed in overt, hostile threats (Dwyer, Osher & Warger, 2000). The main consideration must always be safety for the masses and immediate intervention. Early warning signs of predictive behavior that may lead to violence are identified in figure 7.2.

Identifying a pattern of behavior characteristics with potential for violent acts or danger to others before harm or fatalities occur provides a fundamental step in a tracking system as part of an effective intervention method. Conflict resolution approaches and procedures can be used to track the characteristics and the development of altercations and intervene before tragic results become an irreversible reality.

The basis for determining the success of students, teachers, and programs and must be closely aligned with learning goals and current theories of instruction (Blum & Arter, 1996). Assessment of the conflict

Figure 7.2 Early and Imminent Warning Signs of Violent Behavior

Early Warning Signs	Imminent Warning Signs
Used to help identify and refer individuals whose individual behavior patterns may lead to violence.	*Require an immediate response because potential danger may occur to an individual or to others.*

Early Warning Signs:

- Social withdrawal
- Excessive feelings of isolation and being alone
- Excessive feelings of rejection
- Being a victim of violence
- Feelings of being persecuted
- Low school interest and poor academic performance
- Expression of violence in writings and drawings
- Uncontrolled anger
- Patterns of impulsive and chronic hitting, intimidating, and bullying behaviors
- History of discipline problems
- History of violent and aggressive behavior
- Intolerance for differences and prejudicial attitudes
- Use of drugs and alcohol
- Affiliation with gangs
- Inappropriate access to firearms
- Serious threats of violence

Imminent Warning Signs:

- Serious physical fighting with peers or family members
- Severe destruction of property
- Severe rage for seemingly minor reasons
- Other self-injurious behaviors or threats of suicide
- Threats of lethal violence
- A detailed plan (time, place, and method) to harm or kill others, particularly if the child has a history of aggression or has attempted to carry out threats in the past
- Possession and/or use of firearms and other weapons.

resolution communication program must include an evaluation of critical thinking, problem solving, and communication skills. Collaborative internships with community-based mediation centers and schools produce life-long learning experiences for prospective mediators. By applying conflict resolution education instruction, information, and principles, students are able to analyze disputes and apply their knowledge and skills to help disputing parties find workable solutions to real-life situations. The best assessment approach draws a balance between all the areas being assessed and the reasons for assessing them. The assessment needs to describe student performance well enough so that students and teachers can evaluate progress toward agreed-upon goals. Educators and researchers must continuously look for ways to improve the alignment of assessment content and strategy with proposed changes in curriculum and instruction (Blum & Arter, 1996).

> *The old paradigm assumed that educational opportunities had to be rationed. . . . The new paradigm . . . recognizes that contemporary society is realizing that its members need increasing amounts of school learning. The role of educational evaluation is to help identify the assets of students on which effective educational programs can be built."* *(Blum & Arter, 1996, p. 1–3:3)*

The conflict resolution communication program enables students to apply their knowledge and understanding of mediation techniques and effective communication and coping skills to real-life experiences. Students demonstrate a depth of problem-solving skills and facilitation techniques when placed in community and school-based conflict resolution situations. The mediator integrates program information and conflict resolution education into real-world problems that serve as the "stepping stones to new learning experiences" (Blum & Arter, 1996, p. 1–4:2). A portfolio of the student mediator's personal and instructional goals, accomplishments, self-reflections, activities, and performance as a third-party facilitator provides an integrated performance assessment of the holistic experience. By translating the conflict resolution communication program educational experience into the actual learning experience of real-life conflicts, mediators have a measurement of success or failure, which can also be ascertained by the program head who will be interested in the effectiveness of the program. Feedback to improve or praise the mediator's performance is a valuable assessment tool within the framework for continued professional growth. The development of proposed outcomes affects accompanying changes in educational curriculum, instruction, evaluation, and assessment strategies through numerous meetings, interviews, collaborative and problem-solving sessions with experts and colleagues in related fields. Variance and growth in the program's structure and design will reflect the changing needs of the community.

> *Schools should send the message that those who mistreat others will be dealt with harshly. Children need to know they can rely on their teachers and school administrators to protect them from repeated harassment. And school personnel must pay closer attention to what is going on in the hallways and cafeterias, and keep an eye out for that sullen boy or lonely girl.*
>
> *Our society is less polite and patient than it used to be. We have an irrational sense of outrage and feel justified in meting out punishment to those who wrong us—and we don't always consider the consequences. (Landers, 2001)*

The success of the strategies, techniques, and practices of the conflict resolution communication program depends on a concentrated effort by the entire school community, including parents, teachers, coaches, and staff from the principal to bus drivers as well as all students. Training everyone involved in the prevention of conflict minimizes the chance of violent outbreaks on school property. A recent survey of 15,000 U.S. students conducted by researchers at the National Institutes of Health found that about 30 percent reported they had been perpetrators or victims or both involving school violence (Boodman, 2001, HE 14).

> *The school is a particularly powerful influence. A school that draws clear boundaries to guarantee personal safety and offers a range of programs to support student harmony can help keep student aggression in check. A school that ignores and tolerates bullying inevitably shifts the power from the adults to the peer perpetrators. (Fried & Fried, 1996, p. 103)*

Just as it "takes a village" to raise a child, it takes a whole community to attack violence, loosen its aggressive grasp on the nature of school crime, reroute repetitive and inappropriate behavior patterns, and offer new remedies and solutions for peaceful resolution and negotiation.

Administrators and teachers need to be well informed in the application of conflict resolution communication principles as well as to use those skills in preventing existing conflicts from worsening and turning into tragedies. They need to be able to listen and understand various points of view by the conflicting parties, be heard by all parties, isolate the issues at hand, retrieve facts, and use their expertise when making decisions in the best interests of all concerned. The sensitivity required by trained professional when detecting students with mental and emotional problems extends to recommending the various mediation, anger management, impulse control, mental health resources, and other services for troubled students and their families.

8

Conflict Resolution Communication Techniques for Parents

"You get the best out of others when you give the best of yourself."
— Harry Firestone

Parents serve as role models or examples to their children. Throughout generations, the adult role of caring, providing support, protecting, and teaching our children to survive and to make a good life for themselves and for their families requires planning and goal setting. Sending children to schools excelling in educational opportunities, diligently adding to savings accounts, creating a job hierarchy in family-run businesses, and, often, following in successful parental footsteps becomes the traditional role of the family unit in preparing the next generation to serve the needs of their families and those of society.

The parental role benefits greatly from open communication that begins at birth and offers a lifetime of satisfaction with offspring. Responsibility, truthfulness, tolerance, respect, and an unconditional love must be modeled and passed on to future generations. Saying what we mean and living our lives based on what we express, how we act, and what we feel needs to reveal our principles and the importance we place on communicating honestly and truthfully with one another. Sometimes, however, ambiguity may lead to confusion and miscommunication. A series of misunderstandings, complicated with impatience and harsh words, may become the normal pattern of intervention rather than the exception to the rule. Youthful eyes can often delineate adult actions from words in an atmosphere of puzzled glances, repeated questions, and modeled behavior. Repetitive patterns underlie the actions, gestures, statements, and expressions that form communication. The difficulty arises when, in many cases, the communicator imitates the behavior without recognizing the harm of his or her actions.

When parents can see their children at their worst, and still be able to speak to them knowing who they are at their best, we can free them to move out of the bully role. (Fried & Fried, 1996, p. 78)

More often than not, however, a "disconnect" or a communication breakdown occurs, creating frustration and a sense of misunderstanding between parent and child. The intent to help the adolescent develop and to grow into adulthood with ease and a natural feeling of simplicity, wonderment, curiosity, and perplexity seems suddenly counterbalanced with uncontrolled hormonal changes, powerful temper tantrums, and emotional flairs of anger, irritation, and impatience. Coming of age includes moments of tension, isolationism, despair, and even resentment of parental supervision. The level of information, the sharing of particulars, or dealing with the truth becomes a "now-and-then" occurrence or a "moment-to-moment" conscious effort predicted by the right circumstances. Communication on many levels becomes strained or even nonexistent between parents and their children, and the role model theory and parenting skills become detached from their intended target.

A family divided needs to reestablish a working relationship of valuable interpersonal messaging and verbal correspondence. The quality of relationships in the early years of development sets the stage for later relationships and behavior patterns, which in turn affects the complex communication with teachers, classmates, and authority figures. The experience of the familial connection affects relationship attachments, nurturing guidelines, discipline control, conflict perception, and the way we learn to handle conflict (Fried & Fried, 1996, p. 103). Ingrained patterns of conduct must be understood within the context of establishing and maintaining relevant and vital connections for the betterment of the individual, the family, and society. Patterns of behavior can be amended or adapted as appropriate responses. By listening, hearing, and relating to another's point of view, parents can enable their children to follow patterns of behavior observed with consistency, openness, and effective communication techniques.

Intervention strategies parents can use to bond with their children and help them successfully implement of closer communication strategies include the following tips (Beane, 1999, p. 123):

- Have family discussions and regular home meetings with your child.
- Spend more positive time with your children.
- Encourage children to talk about their experiences.
- Praise your children.
- Limit the amount of violence encountered by your child in video and computer games and found in TV shows and movies.
- Supervise your child's whereabouts and activities closely.
- Consider enrolling yourself and your child in a class on conflict resolution, stress management, anger management, friendship skills, or self-defense.
- Tell your children that you love them and that you will help them work through negative or inappropriate behavior patterns.
- Ask teachers, counselors, and school administrators to keep you informed of your child's behavior at school and work with the school to modify and improve your child's behavior.
- Apply reasonable and appropriate consequences for unacceptable behavior and stay firm.
- Praise your child's efforts to change and follow parental limits and school regulations.
- Seek out parenting classes and professional help if needed.

Conflict resolution communication techniques for parents offer a concise and satisfying bonding experience that links parental counsel to the adolescent demands typical of this age group. (See figure 8.1.) A significant correlation between parental boundaries and the need for teenage recognition, understanding, and exploration of restrictions needs to be acknowledged. The young adult may desire parental guidance and bits of mature wisdom more when it appears less likely to succeed or less likely to be accepted.

Figure 8.1 Conflict Resolution Communication Techniques for Parents

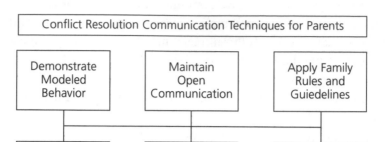

Successful mediation techniques and effective communication skills combine to provide fundamental methods for sustaining a long-term contact between parent and child, for listening to and perceiving the other person's point of view, and for resolving issues and finding solutions to benefit all parties. Conflict resolution communication offers a sense of security within a safe setting that enables a young person to narrate or to express a particular side of the story. Accurate or precise communication affords the participants an opportunity to express their feelings without fear of reprisal or threats of intimidation. The approach that uses feedback or a repetitive exercise of retelling what was heard by one party and relates it to what another party said enables both parties to more effectively reach a mutual understanding. A link is once again formed between parent and child and maintained by adapting effective conflict resolution communication processes as an alternative to destructive behavior and possible violence.

Modeled Behavior

A parent's role should begin as a model for just and tolerant behavior. Parents need to be made aware of physical, verbal, and emotional pressures resulting from sexual abuse or harassment of children or other issues that demean children's self-esteem. In order to help their children, parents need to understand the issues and motives surrounding taunting, bullying, and sexual harassment, and to be ready to help in the following ways (Fried & Fried, 1996, p. 69):

- Understanding the far-reaching impact of sexual harassment on children.
- Being available for offering children advice, support, and understanding.
- Being informed about the normal sexual development stages that children experience.
- Helping children to understand what is appropriate and inappropriate behavior in public and private settings.
- Becoming comfortable with sexual material and establishing an environment that allows for dialogue about sexual feelings, concerns, and fears.
- Ensuring that family experiences create a positive, nontoxic experience.
- Transmitting the important values of anger control, respect for self and others, social skills, and manners, empathy, and responsibility.
- Imposing and respecting consequences that the school invokes.
- Insisting that their child apologize and make amends when warranted.

Children will often reenact their parent's actions, words, and thoughts. Respecting a parent's authority and following appropriate limits will help children to dispel their anger and refrain from taking revenge on innocent parties. Parents need to behave like adults and maintain a sense of calmness in all situations. Learning and practicing simple relaxation techniques when pushed to the edge or taking a "time out" when needed is advisable (Beane, 1999, p. 125). Knowing that the lack of communication can encourage conflicts, misinformation, rumors, threats, and mean-spirited actions on the part of young minds, parents need to "teach their children how hurtful such behavior is, how important it is to stand up for their fellow classmates and how to be a real friend. Parents need to pay attention to what is going on in their children's lives. Parental involvement is the key to a well-adjusted child. Too many parents feel overwhelmed and give up. . . . Get help. Take a parenting class. Find a support group. Do something to ensure the health and safety of your children. Make it your top priority" (*The Washington Post*, Landers, 2001).

Interactive Communication

Interactive and ongoing communication is needed between parents and their children. Being able to transmit thoughts, opinions, and experiences or offer bits of relevant advice also contributes to the listening strategies outlined in the conflict resolution communication process. Deborah Tannen, communication specialist and professor of linguistics at Georgetown University, believes that listening to one another can improve communication in families.

> . . . *But therein lies a key to conversations between adults and teens: To the extent adults have more experience in the world, it is quite right for them to give advice. But to the extent that the world in which teens move is a different one from the world of adults . . . it would be helpful for adults to ask their teenage children to explain (insofar as they can) the world as they see it. After listening and grasping the way this world works, adults will be in a better position to offer advice that might actually be taken.* (Mann, 2001, p. C8)

Family members want to be understood and accepted by one another in a strong atmosphere of bonding and approval. When communication becomes confused, disconnected, and chaotic, the meaning of what is being stated is often not the intended meaning or message as perceived by the listener. Tannen believes:

> *A trick in successful communications is to listen closely to what's being said, and don't leap to emotional conclusions. If we could treat our family conversations with that level of care, we might go a long way toward reducing family strife, discord, and alienation. . . . It is learning*

about talk and the emotions words can produce. It's learning about how to keep peace in the circle of love we hold most dear: our families. (Mann, 2001)

As students learn to develop close relationships with adults—not only with their parents, but also other family and community members—they learn important social skills and build their self-confidence and self-esteem (Beale, p. 105). Sharing problems, accomplishments, social skills, and day-to-day uncertainties is easier when one is able to communicate and be heard by others. Communication practices are an essential connection between parents, children, and school personnel. Taking an active interest in your child and knowing how he or she is doing in school while conferencing with teachers and administrators contributes to sound academic and behavior patterns. Dr. Dan Olweus, a founding father of research on bully/victim problems at the University of Bergen in Norway, encourages this attitude as a means of enhancing the child's overall welfare and school safety. He states that Swedish school policy requires school staff to regularly make contact with parents in the best interests of the child. The official Swedish policy on education states the following (Lgr 80, s. 25), "The school must take it on itself to make contact with the parents to facilitate the necessary cooperation." And, "The responsibility for making sure that contacts are established rests on the school" (Olweus, 1993, p. 94). Once the correlation is made between these two groups, a natural progression of involvement and cooperation needs to be maintained to secure the growth and development of the student. A set of family rules and educational guidelines needs to be addressed and adhered to by the child with a determinate set of consequences in place when violations occur (Olweus, p. 102). (See figure 8.2.)

In a recent *Washington Post* survey that asked parents what they would do to reduce the violence in our schools, the majority of parents responded by wanting to reduce class size as a way to promote a warm environment and a security that comes from everyone being known well by everyone else. Others felt that the parents should be held accountable or liable for their child's behavior "unless the child was in counseling or the parents can prove they were making efforts to get the

Figure 8.2 Reducing School Violence

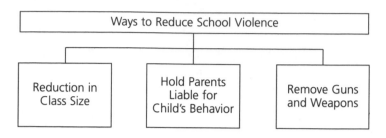

child into counseling at the time the child committed the act of violence." A minority of parents blamed the children directly and others used the issue of school violence as a justification to promote items on their social agendas, such as gun control. Other ideas included the following (Vos Savant, 2001, p. 9):

1. End compulsory attendance at the secondary-school level.
2. Have students wear simple uniforms, such as white shirts and black slacks.
3. Forbid TV to cover school shootings. Our right to information can be satisfied by newspapers. Why reward perpetrators with the splashy attention they seek?
4. Make name-calling, harassing and bullying punishable offenses.
5. Create a 24-hour, toll-free hotline for students to phone in tips.
6. Celebrate achievements other than sports and cheerleading.
7. Consider home schooling.

Parents often take the lead in restoring a better working relationship with their children and a quality of communication to help them better understand the behavior and thinking patterns of their offspring. Being able to be heard and to be understood by adults is a major obstacle for many young people. Conflict resolution communication techniques and strategies help maintain a positive and interactive communication in order to transform future generations into better adult role models who possess effective communication skills and a low propensity for family conflict. Parents are reminded to concentrate on one issue at a time or stay focused on "mini-issues" until progress and clarity are attained. Also, parents must stay in control of the situation but continue to implement communication skills and mediation techniques to diffuse anger and encourage conversation with their children. Parental role model traits and actions are needed to illustrate the effects of patterned behavior in a positive light and at the same time parents must learn to listen to other viewpoints and still be heard and respected by their children.

9

Conflict Resolution Communication Techniques for Students

"To build may have to be the slow and laborious task of years. To destroy can be the thoughtless act of a single day."
— Sir Winston Churchill

The learner is an astonishing "work-in-progress," moving through the years of public education toward a high school diploma. Those years as a student are filled with moments of brilliance, doubt, impatience, anticipation, frustration, credulity, and eagerness in the attempt to absorb overwhelming amounts of knowledge in a short period of time. A student's capacity to store book knowledge has been observed and applauded by those in authority, the same adults who may frequently criticize the student's ability to apply social graces, tolerance, and empathy for others. Students need to know their options when making decisions that affect their future or those of others. Students empowered with a strong sense of right and wrong fare better than peers who surrender their best interest to the whim of their peers (Fried & Fried, 1996, p. 137). They need to be aware of paths that will help ensure success, satisfaction, and recognition. The results of making harmful or violent decisions may not only harm others, but exact an awful price in their own lives.

The conflict resolution communication program enables generations to grow into major decision makers who possess problem-solving techniques and effective coping strategies. Students need to be encouraged to deal with differences and subsequent feelings of anger in positive ways, including the ability to accomplish the following (Fried & Fried, 1996, p. 116):

1. Express anger in words. Learn to communicate using positive statements, including: "It's okay for you to be upset and angry with me for not letting you do what you want, but it's not okay for you to talk to me that way or in that tone of voice."
2. Repeat what you heard and demonstrate an understanding of their feelings.
3. Discuss their reason for being angry. Identify the source of the anger.
4. Cool off, take a time out, and collect your emotions.
5. Exercise or engage in a form of physical activity to release anger.
6. Take deep breaths, listen to soothing music, or concentrate on positive and happy events to secure a calming effect.
7. Find a creative solution.
8. Distract negativity by engaging in a situation requiring your full attention and energy.
9. Share a time when you learned to handle your anger and frustration.
10. Narrate a story, write a poem, or journal to the conflicting party expressing your true feelings and frustrations over the situation and ways to resolve the conflict in a "win-win" format.

The listening and communication guidelines provide an approach that encourages understanding, empathy, and perception to take place before acting without thinking. A system of identifying the issues, tabling the tempered emotions, and acknowledging other points of view can become a routine method to dissolve conflict and evaluate the information. By practicing the principles of conflict resolution communication, students learn to handle situations or altercations in a healthier atmosphere and at the same time promote peaceful resolution and a lifetime of learning.

Unfortunately, some lessons are learned too late by youthful abusers who commit criminal acts of violence. A recent case in point involved a fourteen-year-old student from Lake Worth Middle School in West Palm Beach, Florida, on May 26, 2000. The student was suspended earlier in the day by a school administrator for throwing water balloons. He returned to the school near afternoon dismissal demanding to see two girls in an English class. The 35-year-old male teacher turned the student away who then shot and killed the teacher point blank with a revolver. The youth stated that he had just wanted to scare the teacher, not kill him. In July 2001, the fifteen-year-old youth was sentenced to multiple life sentences with consideration for parole after 35 years. The slain teacher's mother and brother asked the judge to hand down a life sentence, but the teacher's young widow with two small children was unable to give a sentencing recommendation to the court, stating, "I cannot make a recommendation because that is not my job. I do not have the wisdom" (Associated Press, Riddle, July 26, 2001).

The minor was treated as an adult because of the severity of the crime. He showed hardened criminal behavior as well as streaks of violent temper. Somehow, another episode of an angry youth acting out, making life-altering choices for himself and innocent victims, garnering negative attention, and harming society with patterned behavior left its devastating and rippling effects on yet another American school. The warning signs of a possible disturbance by a troubled teen or student needs to be recognized and acted on immediately by a professional trained in conflict resolution communication. (See figure 9.1.)

The significance of the program comes through its potential to teach all students and professionals better communication, mediation, and anger management techniques needed to reduce violence. The program promotes safer schools and communities and helps individuals adopt healthier and more productive means to handle cultural, social, and societal diversity in everyday life.

Figure 9.1 Conflict Resolution Communication Techniques for Students

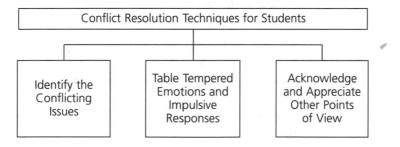

The Echo of Youth

The immediate need for the conflict resolution communication program is evident in national newspapers and on national broadcasts as they reference anniversaries of past acts of violence, such as remembrances of the Columbine High School tragedy in Littleton, Colorado, and identify current eruptions of violent behavior. The following quotes by students demonstrate a relevant concern for effective and immediate intervention:

> When I think about my future I can't really say how school shootings will affect me. I just know it will be hard to explain to my children, but looking at the way things are going, my children will probably already know what school shootings are by the time they're 6. (Kahina Robinson, Duke Ellington School of the Arts, as quoted in Stepp, April 20, 2000)
>
> One year ago, Americans saw a frightening picture on TV: students at Columbine High School fleeing from two teenage shooters, running from their school, their hands over their heads, their faces full of fear. . . . People are questioning whether we really understand the problem of school violence and if we know how to reduce it. The Justice Policy report, meanwhile, recommends a solution that many people agree needs more attention: counseling and anti-violence programs to prevent the problem in the first place. (Shen, April 20, 2000)

School field trips of children visiting the National Zoo in Washington, D.C., to learn, explore, and enjoy their planned study day may have expected anything but fleeing from an armed youngster shooting randomly in a gang-related altercation.

> Yesterday, adults tried to ease the fears of children who read about the Zoo shooting or saw pictures of it on television. . . . President Clinton said yesterday that crime is at a 25-year low, but "our country still has too much violence and too much crime." . . .
>
> "Kids can't do a lot about the climate in a zoo they are visiting, but they can do something about the climate in their own classroom," said

Robert Butterworth, a psychologist who helps children deal with violence. Kids can try to learn peaceful ways to solve arguments, he said, and take action to be peacemakers when they see trouble brewing. (Shen, April 26, 2000)

Students need affirmation, acceptance, and approval by peers, teachers, administrators, parents, siblings, and community members. They need to feel good about themselves and about their own ability to do something positive for themselves and others. Too often, students drift in and out of classes with problems that require attention or special notice by adults or authority figures. A kind word by a teacher who compliments a student or welcomes a student to an English or into a biology class at the beginning of a period is something simple that can make the student feel respected and valued. Student journaling is also a proven way to help students learn to express their feelings and attitudes. The written word becomes a viable form of expression. Positive expression and positive thinking about oneself and others should be encouraged, hopefully inspiring other positive deeds and community service activities. "Positive thinking about ourselves and our abilities to solve problems, reach goals, cope with hard times, and accomplish what we set out to do . . . creates positive beliefs, attitudes, and feelings promoting positive behaviors" (Beane, 1999, p. 68).

Students who volunteered their time, talents, and abilities or became active in community service projects reported the following benefits in a survey conducted by Independent Sector (*Volunteering and Giving Among American Teenagers 12 to 17 Years of Age*, Washington, D.C., 1996):

- Learned to respect others.
- Learned to be helpful and kind.
- Learned how to get along with and relate to others.
- Gained satisfaction from helping others.
- Learned to understand people who are different from them.
- Learned how to relate to younger children.
- Became better people.

- Learned new skills.
- Developed leadership skills.
- Became more patient with others.

If students feel the opportunity to communicate in a safe and trusting atmosphere and contribute their worth to society, anger and hostile feelings will be revealed and exposed constructively with less chance for violence and inappropriate behavior. The key is to counter the factors that show evidence of promoting discipline problems and a propensity for school-related violence among troubled teens. The list includes video games, inappropriate and extreme TV violence, drug use, alcohol abuse, and scars inflicted by parents who are unable to supervise or otherwise meet the needs of their children, unpredictable if not abusive discipline, a lack of encouragement, and plain bad manners. "It sometimes seems as if the patterns that some children arrive [to school] with are branded too deeply to fade" (Perlstein, 2001, p. B7).

Involvement of School Community

Teachers have been known to make lasting impressions on their students, but they are not required or expected to perform daily miracles by dissolving the ongoing violence in American schools. It takes the commitment of the entire community and the principles and resolve demonstrated in the conflict resolution communication process to transform violent patterns of behavior into workable and productive coping strategies and communication models. Only through application of theory, principles, and ongoing practices can young people learn how to solve their differences peacefully. Through such a process, they can learn new ways to interact with others and understand the value and the importance of bridging differences for the improvement of society. (See figure 9.2.)

Students need to listen and appreciate other points of view as well as be heard and understood by others. They must not hesitate to ask for clarification and use examples when needed. Prioritizing issues one

Figure 9.2 Conflict Resolution Communication Transformation Formula

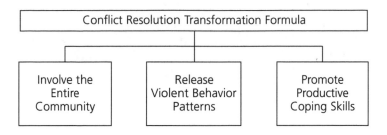

at a time; appreciating and taking advice from parents, teachers, counselors, and friends; choosing options carefully and making appropriate choices; and learning to participate in the fundamental practices of narrative mediation to release personal feelings of blame and guilt are effective conflict resolution communication strategies. The effects of conflict resolution communication can help to heal the wounds of the past and create a quality of life that contributes to a safer world for future generations.

10

Changing Behavior Patterns: The End Is Only the Beginning

"If a man will begin with certainties, he shall end in doubts,
but if he will be content to begin with doubts, he shall end in certainties."
— Francis Bacon in "The Advancement of Learning"

Throughout history, conflicts, wars, and power struggles overshadowed the inherent ability to live in peace with one another. Perhaps, it appeared easier, less complicated, and more efficient to waste human life than to nurture the capacity to reason and to compromise. Perhaps, possible solutions to conflict appeared to be irrelevant attempts to pacify power and control. Perhaps, negotiating differences and learning to live peacefully with one another posed uncertainties and offered only short-lived solutions.

Mediation efforts by the disputants require a commitment and a willingness to make things better for all concerned. The benefit of working together and moving toward reconciliation provides the parties with renewed hope and a sense of direction and strengthens the fabric of coexistence and cooperation. Disagreements and differences can offer an unparalleled opportunity to learn from past mistakes. Assessing the situation, analyzing the problem, narrating the sequence of events, prioritizing and identifying needs, and facilitating possible solutions through the efforts of a neutral third party comprise the components of the conflict resolution communication program. Trained, certified, and degreed mediators using conflict resolution communication techniques can defuse more conflicts and enable individuals to rely on problem-solving skills and communication techniques to solve their differences peacefully.

International negotiator and cofounder of Harvard's Program of Negotiation, Dr. William Ury, urges parties separated by their differences and their disagreements to find peaceful solutions. "Human beings are just as capable of living in peace as they are of living at war with one another. Getting along is perhaps even more rooted in human nature than is fighting to the finish" (Ury, 1999, p. 197). The author champions the power and the process of "Getting to Peace" as a natural way for individuals in distress to resolve conflicts with the aid of a neutral third party (Ury, 1999). An unbiased and nonjudgmental facilitator can guide and direct the negotiation process in a safe and non-threatening environment. Disputants are encouraged to share their feelings and narrate their sequence of events from their particular point of view. Intervention at school, at the workplace, or during a family altercation, requires a mediator who is trained in the fundamental concepts of conflict negotiation and effective communication techniques, and can effectively facilitate agreement between the parties.

The conflict resolution communication program provides this valuable alternative problem-solving service to the community by diffusing conflicts and enabling individuals to better understand themselves and their interaction with others through mediation communication education. Conflict resolution principles and procedures serve as proactive tools and invaluable resources within the community. While Ury emphasizes the will to live peacefully with others, the conflict resolution communication program emphasizes the skills needed to facilitate conflict resolution communication. The bonds of effective cooperation in conflict resolution are strengthened through caring, compromising, and embracing cultural differences and act as a prototype for peaceful negotiations for future generations. (See figure 10.1.)

Changing old patterns of behavior through the use of new coping strategies, listening and communication techniques, mediation procedures, and an acknowledgment or appreciation of universal differences is the first step in a life-long commitment to solving altercations peacefully. Whether at work, at home, at school, or in the community, mutual agreement is an essential ingredient in improving

Figure 10.1 The Benefits of Conflict Resolution Communication

The Benefits of Conflict Resolution Communication		
Promotes New Coping Strategies	Promotes New Behavior Patterns	Promotes New Listening Techniques
Provides a Safe and Trusting Environment	Lessens Violent Behavior Patterns	Enables Critical Thinking and Evaluation Skills

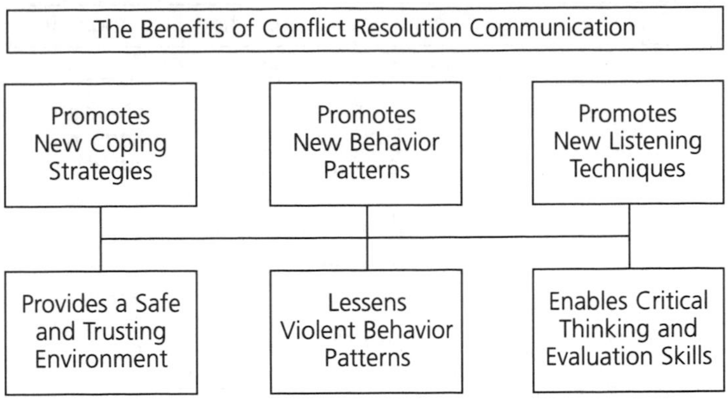

relationships among friends, family, co-workers, or acquaintances and in reducing the perceived need for violence or inappropriate measures.

The transition into new patterns of behavior depends heavily on the use of effective coping skills, identification of issues, removal of emotional baggage, listening and hearing strategies, and stepping into another's point of view. The benefits of conflict resolution communication skills are evident in improved relations with family, friends, and associates at home, in schools, in the workplace, and throughout the community.

Conflict resolution education and effective communication skills provide the necessary strategies to reduce altercations and to promote peaceful solutions. Diffusing heated arguments by identifying issues and setting emotions aside enables the disputants to incorporate the processes and problem-solving skills of mediation, negotiation, and collaboration. (See figure 10.2.)

Modeling and blending conflict resolution education and communication skills facilitates the use of valuable listening and reasoning skills. Analytical thinking, reframing main issues, and empathizing or understanding another's point of view creates an atmosphere of tolerance for successful negotiation and agreement.

Figure 10.2 Conflict Resolution Communication Educational Components

Confict Resolution Communication Educational Components		
Assess Situation	Analyze Problem or Issue	Narrate Sequence of Events
Identify Needs	Prioritize Needs	Facilitate Possible Solutions

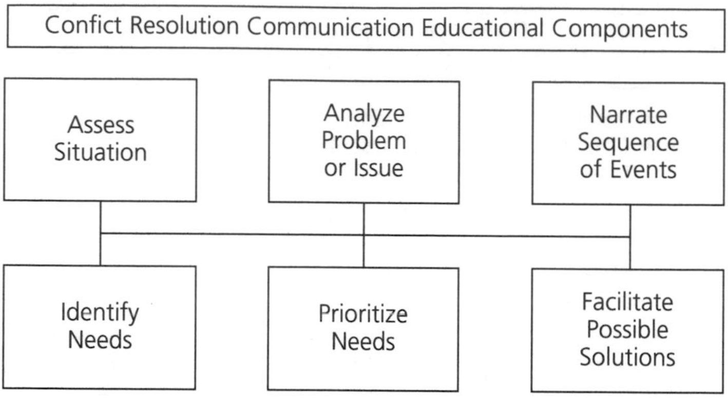

Pattern of Lifetime Learning

The influence of blending communication and mediation skills into a lifetime pattern of choosing effective alternatives to violence remains limitless. By providing the necessary skills and processes for individuals facing difficult situations of inequality coercion, or harassment, individuals can better manage conflicts by using thinking skills to recognize underlying issues. They will have the information at hand to build an arsenal of conferencing techniques to comprehend and receive messages from others and still be able to respond effectively. Early identification and isolation of the issues rather than letting emotions or tempers get out of control contribute to the success of the listening and hearing aspects of conflict resolution communication. Intervention strategies are necessary to break the cycle of repeated behaviors that lead to inappropriate and violent actions. By enabling individuals to build healthier and improved relationships within the family unit, at work, and in the community, for example, conflict resolution communication strengthens a commitment to more peaceful coexistence and models appropriate ways of dealing with diversity.

Effective peacemaking strategies rely on communication techniques in solving problems and brainstorming peaceful outcomes. Old patterns of conduct become useless as new thought processes form creative ways of dealing with conflict and enable a new spirit of trust, respect, and tolerance in adapting to and managing diversity. Conflict resolution communication offers the individual a means to control anger and avert impulse behavior by separating emotions that may include feelings of personal guilt and blame from the actual issue. A re-alignment or reading of verbal and nonverbal cues needs to be addressed by the parties in conflict so that they can communicate the intended meaning of their thoughts and actions and not fall into the potentially harmful outcomes that result from misinterpretation.

The internal causes or reasons for controlling or manipulative behavior patterns need to be revealed, understood, and eradicated to eliminate bullying and other detrimental or hostile acts. Community action and full support of the conflict resolution communication program by administrators, teachers, parents, students, and staff are necessary to effectively implement instructional techniques that will reduce school violence, promote family rules and educational guidelines, and create a safe learning environment. The proactive or preventative nature of conflict resolution communication focuses on addressing cultural and social diversity peacefully, strengthening interpersonal relationships, and enabling individuals to willingly change their behavior patterns by providing alternatives that promote a lifetime of learning without violence.

Epilogue

Sightings for the Future

The fundamental goal and applications of conflict resolution communication education include a life-long learning process focused on reducing violence and implementing appropriate behavior patterns
within human relationships. Old patterns of behavior producing
heated emotions, impulsive outbursts, harsh words, and divided loy-
alties will be diffused as individuals rely on communication skills and
mediation to control the factors that cloud their judgment. Given viable
options and choices to reduce violence and find acceptable paths for
negotiation, people can depend on critical-thinking skills rather than
weapons in resolving inequalities and adapting to cultural diversity.

Children learn effective negotiation, communication, and mediation
techniques by observing behavior as modeled by their parents,
teachers, friends, families, or anyone involved in and finding peaceful
solutions to conflict. Witnessing effective choices that lead to compromise and resolution becomes the best learning device for children
as they grow and develop their own behavior patterns. Eventually,
when conflicting parties come together armed with the skills necessary
to negotiate peacefully, fewer innocent lives will be lost due to actions
committed out of fear, reprisal, and miscommunication. Children will
once again be able to go to school without fearing that they will be shot
or bullied by another student in need of immediate care and professional assistance. Parents can feel a sense of security when dropping
their children off at school or a daycare center and know that steps have
been taken to ensure their safety through the implementation of educational guidelines and conflict resolution communication programs
that reduce violence on school grounds and throughout the community.

TOURO COLLEGE LIBRARY

Imagine for a moment a world filled with less tension, apprehension, and negative behaviors resulting in violence and death and affecting innocent victims and bystanders. Imagine the acceptance of cultural diversity, including the freedom to believe in a personal faith, or the choice to dress in a particular fashion, or the freedom to speak without retaliation. Imagine nations ending years of strife and learning to live with one another in peace. Imagine having the ability to empower individuals, cultures, and nations to effectively change behavior patterns and learn new coping strategies, enhance new ways of communicating, apply problem-solving and brainstorming techniques to conflict, and enable resolutions and agreements through conflict resolution communication.

Afterword

Appreciating Difference:
Mediation for Preventing and Deterring Racism, Sexism, Bullying, and Conflict

By Dr. Jonathan L. Black-Branch, Barrister at One Garden Court, Temple and of Wolfson College, University of Oxford, and Course Tutor of LLM International Law at Oxford Brookes University.

Effective communication and mediation are vital in today's society. Many problems created and perpetuated by misunderstandings result from ineffective communication between individuals. Such problems manifest themselves in the form of racial conflict, harassment, and violence. Such behaviors invariably perpetuate injustice and inequality leading to social exclusion. Tracing the experiences of students, teachers, and community workers in multi-ethnic settings we see that many of these problems can be resolved or indeed prevented in the first instance via mediation and effective communication. We must first identify factors that create and foster racism, sexism, bullying, and violence within the school community and in society at large, then mediate to prevent these incidents.

Toward Understanding

As society becomes increasingly diverse, it experiences a growing need to formulate better understandings as to how children from all backgrounds fit into traditional societal and school structures. Additionally, traditional structures need to foster better understandings, both between and among students from all cultural groups, which will allow

101

all them, parents, and teachers to become full participants in the wider community, regardless of race, religion, gender, or language.

A review of the current literature reveals that even though much written on student needs, very little is actually known about how schools should accommodate and facilitate effective communication and mediation programs to accommodate these same needs. Studies generally concentrate on issues such as managing multicultural resources, institutional responses, curriculum materials, and community and school responses to diversity. These studies are of vital importance for advancing knowledge in the area, but they do not focus on the link between educational practice on a comprehensive level and the more inclusionary practices that effectively prevent racist and sexist behavior as well as address interracial violence and bullying. Systems that embrace and promote school structures aimed at enhancing the creativity of all students and teachers, regardless of gender, ethnicity, religious beliefs, or ethnocultural heritage are needed. Dr. Lincoln's conflict resolution communication model addresses this gap, indeed providing a workable, affordable method of addressing major problems.

More and more, educational policy and decision makers are calling for change. Much of this change is predicated on broadening and deepening understandings of issues pertaining to race, gender, and conflict within school systems. It calls for a deeper analysis of how racism, sexism, and interracial conflict is fostered and perpetuated in the school community. Moreover, schools need methods to deter and prevent such social injustices. The following discussion is divided into three main sections: (1) elements that contribute to sexism, racism, and interracial conflict; (2) strategies to prevent or to deter incidents of sexism, racism, and interracial conflict; and, (3) conflict management pertaining to sexism, racism, and interracial conflict.

Elements That Contribute to Sexism, Racism, and Interracial Conflict

The data collected in a previous study indicate the need for Dr. Lincoln's work at both micro and macro levels. The results show that incidents of racist and sexist behaviors and interracial conflict can be addressed through conflict resolution communication. The five main factors include stereotyping, socialization, misinformation, personal taste, and personal disposition. It should be noted that these five features are inextricably linked, but they are addressed separately to facilitate discussion.

The most prevalent of these elements is stereotyping, which can be attributed to socialization. Moreover, the strongest forces of socialization appear to occur at home and at school. The socialization of stereotyping may be referred to as negative socialization, usually caused by misinformation. It may also be attributed to personal taste and personal disposition. The framework is as follows:

1. Stereotypes
   - Mirroring
   - Parroting
2. Socialization
   - Home
   - School
   - Church
3. Misinformation
4. Personal Taste
5. Personal Disposition

Schools must address these areas in order to assist students in understanding their negative patterns. The following discussion is based on a study previously conducted in the area.

Stereotyping

Staff from all schools in the study stated an awareness of the problems associated with stereotyping. They report it as one of the most common complaints of students. Indeed some administrators admit that the "spin-offs of such behavior" is the root of many of the disciplinary problems they face. Counselors and guidance staff alike report that stereotyping can be attributed to low self-esteem and in some instances alienation suffered by some students. In trying to understand the reasoning behind such behaviors, students tend to mirror and parrot behaviors that, effectively, perpetuate racial and gender stereotypes.

Mirroring

Mirroring is the reproduction of stereotypic images. The student first learns and subsequently mirrors the images they have learned. They subsequently formulate a set of characteristics as to what someone stands for, or represents, based on the stereotype they learned. These images are often quite derogatory and thus perpetuate racist and sexist behaviors.

Shattering the very complex process of mirroring and its sets of preconceived notions of particular classes of people, be they gender or racially based, is done with great difficulty. It may only be achieved by confronting students with evidence that contradicts image they hold. This confrontation must be done in a nonthreatening manner, such as proposed by Dr. Lincoln. They may feel as though their whole world is threatened when they realize that their knowledge base is not only inaccurate, but it is inadequate as well. Effective communication is vital in view of the sensitive nature of this process.

Parroting

Students also exhibit behaviors described as *parroting*. They parrot the behavior they have heard in the past, behavior that has invariably been rewarded and thus they perpetuate it. For example, many students parrot phrases heard in the course of their peer relations. As a result, on at least a surface level, they accept and perpetuate stereotypes, be they related to gender or race. Like mirroring, changing parroting behaviors must be attempted in the least threatening manner possible.

Students themselves admit that they participate in mirroring and parroting stereotyping behaviors. Many do not reflect on the harm they inflict on their fellow students, or even understand why they do it. It seems that they do so because it is a reflex action or an action that may be attributed to socialization. Effective communication can assist students to become critical thinkers who reflect on their actions in order to make more responsible and informed choices.

Socialization

Psychologists and those in the health-care and social work professions write widely on the topic of socialization. It is both a complex and somewhat contested area. It is therefore not the intent of this discussion to explain the socialization process. It is, however, the intent of this study to examine some of the influences that may attribute to the reinforcement of racist, sexist, and bullying behaviors.

Most would agree that socialization consists of a continued reinforcement of certain behaviors. That being the case, it seems inevitable that children also reproduce potentially negative behaviors. The important word in this scenario is *reproduce*. Children mimic their role models in hopes of acceptance. It is this acceptance that reinforces the behavior.

So a student who hears a role model (perhaps his or her hero or idol) making certain claims or comments (be they racist or sexist in nature) is left to believe that, in order to be like the role model, this behavior is accepted and even expected. They thus emulate the hero and repeat the comments. If they are permitted to get away with such behavior, then it becomes reinforced as acceptable behavior.

The child internalizes these behaviors as proper in that he or she receives attention, whether positive or negative, making it more deeply ingrained in his or her value system. Here again, effective communication is vital to dismantling such internalized practices, because many of the behaviors reproduced are based on three important elements, namely, misinformation, personal taste, and personal disposition.

Misinformation

It seems that many students are ill-informed and misinformed about the abilities, talents, and strengths of others. They are not taught sufficiently to appreciate how people are different, nor are they taught how they are also similar. Cultural barriers, in particular, are often difficult to overcome.

Unless people challenge the stereotypes they hear, they are unable to go beyond the racist, sexist, or otherwise biased image they have internalized. A student who hears a negative commentary about certain classes of people, therefore, is more likely to accept it under three conditions.

First, a student is more likely to accept information if he or she is not equipped with the analytical tools required to dispel or question the information received. Self-reflection is vital. Second, the student is more likely to accept the information if he or she is not taught otherwise, that is, if he or she is not taught the reality. And third, the student is more likely to accept the information being presented if it is relayed by his or her role model. The child wants to believe what he or she hears and indeed emulate such behavior. To teach the student the necessary analytical skills to dispel misinformation about people, educators must use a nonthreatening manner, such as developed by Dr. Lincoln.

Personal Taste and Preferences

This discussion would be incomplete without treating the subject of personal taste. We would be naive to think that individuals did not have their own personal tastes and preferences. Some people prefer the color red over blue, others prefer pop/rock music to the opera, and so forth. In that regard, it is only fair to allow a person to exercise his or her personal taste.

The difficulty arises when children develop preferences that are unacceptable based on prejudices against diversity. They may try to present their preferences in terms of dominance over those of other genders or races. Even though it is rather innocuous to allow a student to have a favorite color, a favorite rock group, or indeed a favorite subject in school, the danger arises when he or she is permitted to express his or her preferences in terms of gender or race, particularly when the student actively promotes malice and hatred against others.

At this stage, a personal taste (or preference, as it were) crosses the line into prejudice and discrimination.

No doubt, a fine line can be drawn between one's personal preferences and the actual performance of racially or sexually discriminatory acts. Needless to say, all students and adults, alike, have certain preferences and biases. The main difference between personal preference and discrimination is when one actively encourages her or his feeling to be accepted as the dominant ideology. Many times this tendency is attributed to the manner in which he or she perceives the world and his or her place in it, otherwise called personal disposition.

Personal Disposition

For the purposes of this discussion, the term *disposition* refers to the frame of reference from which an individual views issues. It is similar to personal taste in that it is individual to each person in question, but it is different in that personal taste refers to how one may perceive a specific person, and thus a personal dislike is formed.

Personal disposition, on the other hand, is more deeply rooted in one's personality. It is their dominant view of the world at large including their epistemological beliefs and values, which are formatively linked to socialization. Some children, for example, are much more happy-go-lucky, while others at the other end of the continuum are more guarded and skeptical about people. And then, of course, most people fall in between these two extremes. The ones who are more cynical sometimes give other people a difficult time and are more difficult to deal with. This difficulty is often manifested in racist and sexist behaviors.

Strategies to Prevent or Deter Incidents of Sexism, Racism, and Interracial Conflict

Educators generally agree that, regardless of the contributing factors behind racist or sexist behaviors, such behaviors are inappropriate and must not be tolerated under any circumstances within the school community. The findings of the study indicate that the following guidelines will assist in preventing and deterring racist and sexist behaviors, in accordance with the nonthreatening manner described throughout Dr. Lincoln's work.

These guidelines describe actions used in the conflict resolution process to socialize students into different behaviors by providing correct information to students and by helping them develop analytical tools to evaluate situations and reach their own conclusions rather than blindly follow role models. It is hoped that such strategies will encourage students to be reflective and assess their own behaviors as responsible critical thinkers rather than fall into the hegemonic reproduction of stereotypes and negative socialization.

Effective Communication and Mediation Guidelines

1. Encourage students to question stereotypes. Challenge them to think critically about what they hear rather than mirror and parrot without questioning what they are doing and why they are doing it.
2. Encourage them to question their preconceived notions of particular classes of people and groups of people, be they gender or racially based.
3. Assist students in recognizing stereotypes. Encourage them to shatter any biased mirror images they have learned.
4. Discourage students from making sweeping generalizations. Help them see individual differences between and among people.
5. Encourage contact with the home and discussion of any concerns that may be established or reinforced at home. Assist students to see beyond certain stereotypes or generalizations that are being emphasized at home.
6. Encourage open dialogue with students at school. Assist them in reaching broader understandings of issues relating to gender, race, and conflict.
7. Encourage positive school interactions. Assist students in exhibiting positive actions and conforming to appropriate behaviors.

Teach the appropriate behaviors and work patiently to reinforce attitudes that will prevent and eliminate inappropriate actions and inappropriate verbal responses.

8. Encourage positive peer interactions. Assist in developing appropriate social behaviors by modeling ones that are exemplar.
9. Provide accurate information about subjects of discussion, making a point to identify misinformed students to correct their error, and inform them.
10. Teach the difference between personal taste and the application of sweeping generalizations about groups of people.
11. Assist students to distinguish between personal preferences and reinforcing stereotypes.
12. Encourage students to be positive, and challenge them to overcome any negative personal dispositions.
13. Educate students who are at the receiving end (the victims) of bullying, personal dislikes, or negative personal dispositions to protect themselves from such antisocial behaviors by not internalizing these comments. Help them to realize that sometimes people project their problems onto others in an inappropriate manner.
14. Teach children that all people are equal and to extend the same level of dignity to others that they themselves would want or expect.
15. Do not reward negative behaviors. Work on developing them into positive features. Conversely, do not allow positive behaviors to go unrewarded, but make sure they are reinforced.

School Policy and Practice: A Call for Consistency

Policies and practices vary from school board to school board and even within boards. This inconsistency extends even within individual schools. Although some teachers promote the principles on the preceding list, not all teachers share equally in the responsibility. It seems to vary from one school to the next, based on both the board of education in question and the local school itself.

Some schools integrate these principles widely across the curriculum, emphasizing it as the responsibility of all teachers, in all subject disciplines, to incorporate these principles into their everyday teachings and routines. Other schools, however, are more scattered in their policies. Individual teachers take seriously the task of presenting these principles in their daily lessons, and others reportedly do so rarely or never.

As a result, students in schools with inconsistent policies on racist and sexist strategies report receiving mixed messages as to what is expected and indeed accepted within the broader school community. These students learn how to avoid problems by acting out the expectations as they perceive them in relation to specific teachers. They do not internalize the values of nondiscrimination. They simply learn when and where to say and do that which is expected of them.

Students in schools that espouse antidiscrimination policies across the curricula, however, are very different. It seems that most of these students adopt and internalize such values. They are more confident as to what is expected of them and what is accepted within the school community. Moreover, they carry these values beyond the schoolhouse door and into society at large.

Conflict Management Pertaining to Sexism, Racism, and Interracial Conflict

An effective means of dealing with the negative behaviors that are manifested in the form of racial and gender harassment is essential. First, school staff and educators must encourage the victims of such antisocial behaviors to come forward and report such incidents. Students must have both faith and trust in their school system. Second, school administration must be committed to dealing with such behaviors in both a professional and decisive manner as proposed by Dr. Lincoln.

When issues are dealt with properly, a twofold change of culture occurs within the school community, making it a more healthy and productive environment. First, by dealing directly with issues of racism and sexism, the victims of such harassment will feel more secure about their positions within the school community. They will receive the clear message that issues of this nature will be addressed. Second, it will send the unequivocal message to those who are victimizing others that racist, sexist, and bullying behavior is not tolerated.

It stands to reason, therefore, that students will be less likely to victimize others simply because they know that discipline by school authorities will follow. Such an environment creates an incentive for students to come forward and report incidents of racial and sexual harassment, which also serves as a deterrent to those who perpetuate such negative behaviors. The following list offers a few suggestions for promoting this type of positive school culture.

Effective Communication Guidelines

1. Establish both formally structured and informal channels for dealing with students who display inappropriate behaviors.
2. Encourage students who are subjected to inappropriate behaviors to pursue the appropriate channels for dealing with these matters.
3. Discourage the exchange of words or force between individuals in order to prevent an escalation of the further problem.
4. Create policies for dealing with students who are identified as perpetuating stereotypes. Early detection is important.
5. Encourage students who are subjected to racist and sexist stereotypes to pursue the appropriate channels for dealing with these matters. Once again, discourage the exchange of words between individuals or the exchange of force.
6. Make it abundantly clear that the school will act on complaints regarding inappropriate behaviors and stereotyping to encourage those who have been perpetrated against to come forward and hopefully deter those who are perpetrating such inappropriate behaviors.
7. Educate students to understand that issues of racism and sexism are everybody's concern and are not to be tolerated under any circumstances. This message must be succinct and unambiguous.
8. During any instance of physical confrontation, separate those involved and have them sit in separate rooms until the situation

calms down. Having them remain in the same room may only serve to escalate the situation. Face-to-face discussions may occur in due course, if deemed appropriate in that particular situation.

9. Allow students an opportunity to explain their side of the story. Denying them the opportunity to speak may only compound their frustration. Let them participate in the process, but remember that participation does not mean an acquiescence of responsibility.

10. Teach students management of anger, including strategies for controlling or containing their anger.

11. Teach courses pertaining to crises management. Assist teachers in developing strategies for controlling or containing crises situation.

12. Teach students and staff skills in conflict management. Assist them in developing strategies for dealing with situations before they escalate out of control.

Preventative Measures

Regardless of how reactive a school is prepared to be in relation to racist and sexist behaviors, it is essential to remember that prevention is always the best remedy. A proactive approach is illustrated by Dr. Lincoln's conflict resolution communication program.

Calling for a Holistic School/Community Communicative Approach

Conflict resulting from racism, sexism, bullying, and interracial tension induces a number of adverse effects on people (including teachers, parents, and students). Research indicates that conflict causes frustration and impatience (Kahn et al., 1964); anxiety (Chinoy, 1987); low tolerance (Miles & Petty, 1975); and even burnout (Crane & Iwanicki, 1987).

Indeed, the study on which this discussion is based indicates that racist and sexist behaviors lower self-esteem. It is widely accepted that low self-esteem leads to failure in school. Moreover, many problems in education are directly related to feelings of self-worth as a person. Developing positive self-esteem in children leads to success in school, which inevitably carries throughout life. This study indicates that racism, sexism, and bullying not only lower self-esteem, but perpetuate injustice and social inequities both in the classroom and in the community at large. In addition, they reinforce a host of negative antisocial behaviors in the perpetrator.

As society becomes more and more pluralistic, a definite need to work toward eliminating racism, sexism, and bullying harassment emerges. Formulating better understandings as to why children in school perpetuate racist and sexist attitudes and violence begins with the need to change negative behaviors.

Combating these behaviors on one or two fronts would be largely ineffective. Racism and sexism must be dealt with on a large scale by implementing a variety of approaches on a number of different fronts. All educators must take a stand and deal with all instances of inappropriate behaviors in a holistic fashion. A holistic school community approach toward eliminating racism and sexism in schools is taken in the broader context of the entire community and includes racism and sexism awareness across the curricula. It is the responsibility of all teachers, in all subject areas, in all schools, in all boards of education, in all states.

It requires leadership development at every level—government, board and within local schools. It affects administrators, teaching staff, parents, and students. This type of network of cooperation within the whole community, involving parents as well as educators, is referred to as *contributory alliance*. Educators work toward an alliance with the entire community to effectively address and indeed eliminate racist, sexist, and bullying behaviors. Education plays a pivotal role in such a contributory alliance, which is best fostered through effective communication and mediation. The Lincoln model of conflict resolution communication is vital to this process.

References

Anderson, P. A. (1999). *Nonverbal communication: Forms and functions.* Mountain View, CA: Mayfield Publishing Company.

Beane, A. L. (1999). *The bully free classroom.* Minneapolis, MN: Free Spirit Publishing, Inc.

Blum, R. E., & Arter, J. A. (1996). *A handbook for student performance assessment in an era of restructuring.* Alexandria, VA: Association for Supervision and Curriculum Development.

Bodine, R., & Crawford, D. (1998). *The handbook of conflict resolution education.* San Francisco: Jossey-Bass Inc.

Bodine, R., Crawford, D., & Schrumpf, F. (1994). *Creating the peaceable school: A comprehensive program for teaching conflict resolution.* Champaign, IL: Research Press.

Boodman, S.G. (June 5, 2001). "Teaching bullies a lesson." *The Washington Post,* p. HE 12.

Cohen, A. M., & Brawer, F. B. (1989). *The American community college.* San Francisco: Jossey-Bass Inc.

Conflict Resolution Education Network (CREnet). (2000). *Conflict resolution education facts.*

Department of Education. (April 28, 2000). *Riley, Reno issue action guide for safeguarding America's children.* Press release, Washington, D.C.

Department of Justice. ERIC Document Reproduction Service No. ED 418 372.

Dority, B. (1999). The Columbine tragedy: Countering the hysteria. *The Humanist, 59*(i4), p. 7.

Duranti, Allesandro. (1994). *From grammar to politics.* London: University of California Press.

Dwyer, K., Osher & Warger, C. (Spring 2000). *Early warning, timely response: A guide to safe schools.* Washington, D.C: U.S. Department of Education.

Eisenberg, A. M. & Smith, R. R. (1971). *Nonverbal communication.* Indianapolis, IN: Bobbs-Merrill.

Fried, S. & Fried, P. (1996). *Bullies and victims.* New York: M. Evans and Company, Inc.

Gallup, G. (1998). *The Gallup poll: Public opinion 1998.* Wilmington, DE: Scholarly Resources Inc., (pp. 60–61).

"The incredible shrinking crime rate." (January 11, 1999). *U.S. News & World Report, 126*(il), p. 25 (1).

Knapp, M. L. & Hall, J. A. (1997). *Nonverbal communication in human interaction.* 4th edition. Fort Worth: Harcourt Brace College Publishers.

Kritek, P. B. (1994). *Negotiating at an uneven table.* San Francisco: Jossey-Bass Inc.

Landers, A. (2001). Ann Landers. *The Washington Post.*

Leeson, S. M., & Johnston, B. M. (1988). *Ending it: Dispute resolution in America—Descriptions, examples, cases, and questions.* Cincinnati, OH: Anderson.

"Man kills 7 children in school rampage in Japan." (June 8, 2001). *The Washington Post.*

Mann, J. (June 22, 2001). "Listening first can improve communication in families." *The Washington Post,* p. C8.

"Numbers." (May 3, 1999). *Time, 153*(il7), p. 19 (1).

Olweus, R. (1993). *Bullying at school: What we know and what we can do.* Oxford, England: Blackwell Publishers.

Perlstein, L. (2001). "Schools awash in bad behavior." *The Washington Post.*

Riddle, A. (July 26, 2001). "Slain teacher's brother, mom testify." Associated Press.

Scott, G. G. (1990). *Resolving conflict with others and within yourself.* Oakland, CA: New Harbinger Publications, Inc.

Smith, M. (1993). Some school-based violence prevention strategies. *NASSP Bulletin, 77*(557), p. 70 (6). Reston, VA: National Association of Secondary School Principals.

Stern, L. (September 1, 2001). "Heading off violence." *Woman's Day.*

"Teacher killed in Florida school shooting." (May 26, 2000). Reuters Wire Service.

U.S. Department of Education and Justice. (2000). *Putting it all together: An action plan, 7*(1), pp. 2–3. The Eric School Safety Review.

U.S. Department of Justice. (March 1999). *The Clinton administration's law enforcement strategy: Combating crime with community policing and community prosecution taking back our neighborhoods one block at a time.* Washington, D.C., pp. 1–8.

Vos Savant, M. (August 12, 2001). "Ask Marilyn." *The Washington Post.*

West, R., & Turner, L. (2000). *Introducing communication theory: Analysis and application.* London: Mayfield Publishing Company.

Winslade, J., Monk, G., & Cotter, A. (1998). A narrative approach to the practice of mediation. *Negotiation Journal, 14*(1), pp. 21–39.

Winslade, J., & Monk, G. (2000). *Narrative mediation: A new approach to conflict resolution.* San Francisco: Jossey-Bass, Inc.

Yarn, D. H. (1999). *Dictionary of conflict resolution.* San Francisco: Jossey-Bass, Inc.

Index

About the Author

Melinda Lincoln holds two bachelor's degrees, one in secondary education from California University of Pennsylvania and another in paralegal studies from the University of Maryland. She received her master's degree in teaching in 1998, attended the University of Oxford in England as a resident doctoral student in the Honors Doctoral Study Abroad Program in 1999, and received her doctorate in education and communication from George Mason University in 2001. Her studies focused on education, sociolinguistics, legal communication, and mediation. She spoke at the Oxford Brookes School of Law on effective communication and mediation techniques applied by prominent U.S. and British women in the area of human rights and politics and received her mediation certification from the National Center for Mediation Education. She has attended postdoctoral seminars at the Johns Hopkins School of Public Health and Hygiene on international perspectives on youth violence and participated in doctoral seminars at George Mason University, where she received the 2001 Graduate School of Education Distinguished Program and Community Service Award for the creation and implementation of her conflict resolution communication program, which is aimed at resolving differences peacefully and training more mediators.

Her recent publications include "Conflict Resolution Education: A Solution for Peace," published in *Communications and the Law, A Quarterly Review* (March 2001), "Negotiation: The Opposing Sides of Verbal and Nonverbal Communication" published in the *Journal of Collective Negotiations in the Public Sector* (July 2001), and "Conflict Resolution Communication: A Solution for Peaceful Co-Existence," published in the *Community College Journal*, December/January, 2002–2003 issue, American Association of Community Colleges.

Dr. Lincoln is currently a professor of communication at George Mason University in Fairfax, Virginia, an educational mediation coordinator, and a senior English teacher for the Fairfax County public school system. Her twenty years of teaching experience included assignments for the Montgomery County public schools, Prince William county public schools, and the Baltimore County public school system. Her motivational speaking events at elementary, middle, and high schools focus on the benefits, techniques, and strategies of conflict resolution communication education, which shows students, parents, teachers, and administrators how to deal with conflict without resorting to violence or inappropriate behavior. She is a current member of the Phi Delta Kappa International Society, an associate member of the Association for Conflict Resolution, and the recipient of the Fulbright Teacher and Administrator Exchange Award by the U.S. Department of State for the academic year 2002–2003 in England.

About the Contributors

Gustavo A. Mellander, Ph.D., is Professor of Educational Leadership, College Administration, and Dean Emeritus at the Graduate School of Education at George Mason University in Fairfax, Virginia. Dr. Mellander earned his Ph.D. from The George Washington University. He also received a Doctor of Humane Letters from Felician College. He was selected to attend the American Council on Education's Institute for Academic Deans and later its Institute for College Presidents. He is also a graduate of the AACTE Institute for Deans of Colleges of Education.

He served as a faculty member, a department chair, a division chair, a university dean for six years, a president for ten years, a district chancellor of a two-college district with a student body of 35,000 for seven years, and a graduate dean for five years. He also served as a dean of business affairs and a university chancellor in interim capacities. He is a charter faculty member of a national institute created to train college presidents. Dr. Mellander helped establish several doctoral programs and taught doctoral leadership courses at Lehigh and Inter American Universities. He also lectured doctoral candidates at Columbia, Seton Hall, and Fairleigh Dickinson Universities as well as at the University of Puerto Rico on the role of educational leaders. He served on 53 high school and college accreditation teams and as a consultant to numerous school districts and colleges. In 1994 he co-authored *The Community College Presidency*. His present research interests include the role of educational leaders, how schools and colleges transform themselves, and classroom teachers as leaders.

As director at the New Jersey Department of Higher Education, he exercised academic program approval and financial overview for 38 colleges and universities. He worked closely with 38 presidents, their university boards, and the state board of education. He helped write higher education and secondary education legislation. Later he developed statewide implementation guidelines. Dr. Mellander served on ACE's New Jersey Panel for the Advancement of Women in Higher Education. He is a founding member of the American Association of University Administrators and was elected to the association's first board of trustees. He also served on a city school board, a state board of education, on several college boards and national commissions. He chaired a governor-elect higher education transition team. He established Latin American Studies departments at three universities and wrote several books on Latin America, including the critically acclaimed *The United States in Panamanian Politics.* He has also written books on Malaysia and Singapore, U.S. history, and college presidents. He is presently the Washington correspondent for The Hispanic Outlook in Higher Education.

Dr. Jonathan Black-Branch holds two Doctor of Philosophy Degrees from the University of Oxford and the University of Toronto. He obtained his Master of Arts Degree in Law from the University of Oxford and his Bachelor's Degree from Oxford Brookes University. He rounded off his post-graduate studies in law at Harvard University and in French Literature at the Université of Nice.

Currently, Dr. Black-Branch is a Barrister-at-Law in London, a member of the Honourable Society of Lincoln's Inn of Court, a professor at Wolfson College, University of Oxford, and Director of the Graduate School of International Law at Oxford Brookes University. He currently serves as a member of the Chartered Institute of Bankers and the Chartered Institute of Arbitrators. He received the Queen Elizabeth II Silver Jubilee Medal for "worthy and devoted services to the Community" and the St. John's Grand Prior's Award. Dr. Black-Branch has authored six books, more than thirty-five referenced journal articles, and more than fifty chapters, conference papers, and reports. He currently travels to the Middle East to hold mediation conferences and negotiation sessions between the Israelis and the Palestinians with a team of expert arbitrators from the University of Oxford.